"This high quality book, *We Speak*, won't quite fit in my hip pocket, but it does for my ministry what my Leatherman does for important fix-it jobs. This book is rich in both theological truths and practical application. From the words of a lowly quartet of lepers to the lofty proclamations of kings, *We Speak* reminds the reader of the power and importance of the words we are compelled to share about our faith. And if that wasn't enough, there is the added bonus of a small group study included. I'm confident you will gain as much from this great tool as I have."

Tom Ellsworth, senior pastor, Sherwood Oaks Christian Church, Bloomington, IN, author of *Beyond Your Backyard* and *Inverted*

"God has given each of us a very unique gift—our voice. Nobody can speak for us but us. In *We Speak* we are reminded of both the necessity and privilege of letting our voice be heard. There is a time, place and manner of speaking that maximizes what people hear us say. This is a great read for anyone who wants to make the most of their words."

Cal Jernigan, senior pastor, Central Christian Church of Arizona

"*We Speak* is a strong call to evangelism, but it's not about guilt, tracts, or fire and brimstone. This book will remind you that the good news about Jesus is worth telling, but it will also help you know what to say and how to say it."

Kyle Idleman, teaching pastor, Southeast Christian Church, Louisville, KY, and author of *Not a Fan*

"*We Speak* offers a heartfelt challenge for Christians to proclaim the story of Christ with courage and boldness. Mike Baker's passion for the preaching of the Gospel—whether in a pulpit before thousands or over coffee with a friend—drips from every page, carrying the reader through chapter after chapter of insight, encouragement and instruction about becoming 'dangerous witnesses' for Christ. . . . *We Speak* will advance the kingdom by challenging and equipping even the most complacent, the most tentative and the most passionate of believers to enter the conversation of our culture with the heart of Christ, the empowerment of the Spirit and the message of salvation."

Daniel Overdorf, dean of the School of Congregational Ministry, Johnson University

We Speak

PROCLAIMING TRUTH IN AN AGE OF TALK

Mike Baker, J. K. Jones
and Jim Probst

IVP Books

An imprint of InterVarsity Press
Downers Grove, Illinois

InterVarsity Press
P.O. Box 1400, Downers Grove, IL 60515-1426
ivpress.com
email@ivpress.com

InterVarsity Press® is the book-publishing division of InterVarsity Christian Fellowship/USA®, a movement of students and faculty active on campus at hundreds of universities, colleges and schools of nursing in the United States of America, and a member movement of the International Fellowship of Evangelical Students. For information about local and regional activities, visit intervarsity.org.

Cover design: Cindy Kiple
Interior design: Beth McGill
Images: Abstract white speech bubble: © Kumer/iStockphoto

ISBN 978-0-8308-4425-8 (print)
ISBN 978-0-8308-9862-6 (digital)

Printed in the United States of America ∞

 As a member of the Green Press Initiative, InterVarsity Press is committed to protecting the environment and to the responsible use of natural resources. To learn more, visit greenpressinitiative.org.

Library of Congress Cataloging-in-Publication Data
Baker, Mike, 1965 February 1-
We speak : proclaiming truth in an age of talk / Mike Baker, J.K. Jones and Jim Probst.
*   pages cm*
Includes bibliographical references.
*   ISBN 978-0-8308-4425-8 (pbk. : alk. paper)*
1. Witness bearing (Christianity—Prayers and devotions. I. Title.
BV4520.B258 2015
248.5—dc23

                                    2015013545

P	20	19	18	17	16	15	14	13	12	11	10	9	8	7	6	5	4	3	2	1
Y	32	31	30	29	28	27	26	25	24	23	22	21	20	19	18	17	16	15			

The authors humbly dedicate this book

to the fearless Christ-followers at Eastview Christian Church.

We are grateful that you allow us to speak into your lives,

but we are more grateful for how you speak into ours.

Contents

Introduction

On April 13, 1829, Alexander Campbell walked onto the stage of a 1,200-seat Methodist Church in Cincinnati, Ohio, to debate the well-known socialist and agnostic Robert Owen. This famous encounter lasted for over one week, during which time each man gave at least twenty-five individual speeches in front of standing-room-only crowds. In one of these exchanges, the articulate Campbell is said to have given a twelve-hour speech "explaining the rationale for Christianity."[1] And people stayed! This is not the only debate Campbell is known to have participated in, but this is the primary one in which he clearly articulated a defense for faith in Christ in a compelling and influential way.

Campbell did not just speak through debate, however. He was arguably the leading voice in seventeenth-century America for what has come to be known as the Restoration Movement. Along with Barton Stone, he led a grassroots movement of independent Christian churches as an itinerant preacher, covering much of the East Coast and Midwest on horseback. He was also a very influential writer as the primary contributor for two publications. For about seven years he published the *Christian Baptist*, but his greatest work in publication came later in life when he edited and published the *Millennial Harbinger* from 1830 to 1863.[2] He also established Bethany College in 1840, serving as both professor and president, adding his voice to the world of Christian education.

Obviously, Campbell made a lasting impact, but most of us are not historical figures nor do we have the opportunities he had. Some of us have an official voice in the church through preaching, teaching, leading or writing, but most Christians never find themselves in front of an audience in the traditional sense. Even if we were all equally gifted as public speakers, there is no longer much interest in debates, and fewer and fewer Americans are attending church regularly, if at all.

Yet this fact remains: as Christians, we are called to speak.

Our times and places in history may vary, and our audiences may not be equal in size, but we are all called to add our voice to the conversation. Why? Because Jesus himself has commissioned each of us to be a witness for his kingdom. And every believer has a faith testimony—a story of how Jesus has made all the difference—compelling us to be his representatives. It's not someone else's job to do the talking for Christ. No, in the church, we all speak. We pray that this book challenges and encourages you to join the conversation and helps you identify your voice in the process.

Speaking of voices, there are three that you will hear throughout this book. All the chapter content was written by Mike Baker, while J. K. Jones authored the five daily devotional readings at the end of each chapter. At the back of the book you'll find a weekly small group guide by Jim Probst. You may also want to view the companion videos, which are available separately. These resources are designed to reinforce the themes of the book and to invite you into the conversation.

In the next few pages, we will be inspired by the boldness and resolve displayed in the lives of the early believers who claimed they couldn't help but speak. All generations will be motivated to speak, as both young and old will find unique ways to enter the conversation. Along the way, we'll be convicted by some Old Testament lepers who learned that they couldn't keep good news to themselves, and we'll empathize with a powerful prophet who went largely unheard. Surprisingly, we will find that our voices are most powerful when we are weak and that our hope is strengthened in times of intense persecution.

More than anything, we will all be reminded that the church still has a message and that we are the voices that carry it.

We are called to speak of

- a God who holds it all together;
- the salvation won through Jesus' death, burial and resurrection;
- the hope of eternal life;
- peace, love, grace and forgiveness; and
- the living Word, Jesus.

We have experienced the Word. His Spirit testifies through us of the Word. Our Savior has commanded us to spread the Word. The world needs the Word now more than ever. And so . . . we speak.

one

We Cannot Help But Speak

People are talking—in every moment of every day, in every part of this world. Talking is one of the most natural expressions of the human reality, and at this point in history we have more ways to express ourselves than ever before.

Social media is at the leading edge of communication in this culture. Through the Internet phenomenon called Facebook, we communicate with "friends" by updating our status, posting photos and comments, and giving our approval by simply clicking "Like." Over 728 million people a day speak using this medium. For more succinct conversations, millions more limit themselves to 140 characters while communicating to their followers on Twitter. Texting is also used to relate information in short, unpunctuated phrases. And in an even briefer messaging form, a person can simply post a photo on Snapchat. Maybe a picture *is* worth a thousand words.

Aside from speaking through electronic means, we also speak the old-fashioned way on occasion. People still use their cell phones for conversation, often hands-free with headphones so they appear to be talking to themselves. And of course, people talk face-to-face in every public and private setting imaginable. We talk to coworkers around the office microwave, to family and friends over a meal at home or restaurant and to strangers in the checkout line or walking down the street.

So, what is everyone talking about? If billions of people are talking simultaneously every minute of every day on planet Earth, what is the content of those conversations? Some of it is strictly informational, like giving directions to a desired location or teaching someone how to do something. Sometimes words are used to express emotions that range from anger to love. Mostly, however, our conversations are filled with the sharing of life experiences. We talk about the stuff that happens to us. We communicate what we've done. We relate what our senses take in. We speak about what we have seen and heard.

It was the same in the first century.

The Talk in Jerusalem

An event that takes place in the early life of the church gives us an example of how we communicate the circumstances of life. In chapters 3 and 4 of Acts, we find that everyone in Jerusalem is talking about the same thing, and these conversations are the backdrop for our first speaking lesson. As we eavesdrop on this Bible dialogue, we will gain some important insight into our twenty-first-century dialogue as followers of Christ.

Peter and John were simply doing what any good Jewish person living in first-century Jerusalem would. It was time for the afternoon prayers, and they were headed to the temple to pray. If you're surprised that they were continuing in this Old Testament tradition, you shouldn't be. Yes, they were followers of Jesus, but they saw him as the fulfillment of the Law and the Prophets, not a competitor. So they were going to pray when they encountered a lame man who sat at the gate he had begged at for years. They must have experienced this many times before. We don't know much about this man except that he couldn't walk, that his friends probably carried him to that same spot every day and that he was looking for a handout. Soon he would be the focus of every conversation in town.

It's obvious that the man didn't expect much from two peasant apostles from Galilee because he wasn't even looking their way when he made his customary plea. Peter, however, made eye contact with him and told him he couldn't give him any money, but he could give him something better. Boldly he declared that the man was healed in the name of Jesus and reached out his hand to help him up. Suddenly, the lame man felt power surge into his feet and ankles, and miraculously he was standing on his own. His eyes widened. His heart pounded with excitement. He cautiously took a few steps. Then he walked. Then he jumped up and down. Then he skipped through the temple courts, loudly praising God and sharing the news with anyone who would listen.

This caused quite a stir in the solemnity that usually accompanied the time of prayer. People glanced at the spectacle caused by this dancing worshiper. When they recognized who it was, they stared, then they whispered, then they followed him. A miracle had taken place, and the news quickly spread from the temple to the busy streets to the marketplace and eventually to the home of the high priest. An impromptu gathering of hundreds now pushed close to get a glimpse of the man and his healers.

The lame man had a testimony. The people of Jerusalem had something to talk about. Peter and John had an audience. And the Jewish leaders had a problem. Together we can learn about our speaking by examining what each of these individuals or groups was saying.

People talk about the exceptional things that happen but most of life is mundane. Getting dressed, brushing teeth, putting on makeup, driving to work, sitting in class, fixing dinner, taking out the trash and doing dishes are just a few of the daily acts that make up the routine of our lives. We normally don't talk much about these things because, well, everyone does them, and no one cares if you do them. You don't often hear a thirty-year-old exclaim to her coworkers, "Guess what! I brushed my teeth this morning." This is "who cares" stuff—the kind of information that annoys us when it occasionally gets posted on Facebook and Twitter. The stuff of everyday is just not that interesting and really isn't worth talking about.

What gets our attention and creates conversation is the out of the ordinary and the completely unexpected. If you find a hundred dollars while you're brushing your teeth, that's something to talk about. If you lose a tooth while brushing your teeth, you've got some fodder for conversation. If you accidentally brush your teeth with sunscreen, go to the doctor—and you have a story to tell. What's true now about having something to say has always been true with people, and it was true in the book of Acts. It's the exceptional that we talk about, and the healing of this lame man was exceptional.

Going to the temple at three in the afternoon was not a story for those Jerusalem worshipers. Most of them were there every day at the morning and evening times of prayer. The Scriptures read by the rabbis and the prayers recited by the priests were "as usual." The smell of incense, the bleating of goats, the Levite choir singing, the clanging of coins in the treasury boxes, blah, blah, blah. No news here. But then some shabbily dressed, unshaven guy comes running and leaping through the courts yelling, "Hallelujah!" at the top of his lungs. Now we have a story. And when we find out who this worshiping maniac is, we really have something to talk about.

The Scriptures describe the scene for us. "All the people saw him walking and praising God, and recognized him as the one who sat at the Beautiful Gate of the temple. . . . And they were filled with wonder and amazement at what had happened to him. . . . All the people [were] utterly astounded" (Acts 3:9-11). Picture people today tweeting, "At the temple, just saw a lame man walk by #miracle #crazy." A video of the man walking goes viral on YouTube, and the lame man updates his status.

These early witnesses didn't have our technology, but they did have something to converse about. Friends asked one another if they had just seen what they thought they had. Others raced home to tell their families. Some heard the commotion and pieced the story together from several sources. Soon the entire population of Jerusalem had heard about the miracle and gathered around the main characters: the apostles Peter and John, with the healed man nearby. This was their chance to speak, and speak they did.

Address Your Audience

Notice how this witness opportunity came about. Speaking for Jesus, then and now, is arranged by the Holy Spirit through events and circumstances in our lives. There is no evidence that Peter and John were going to the temple on that particular day to do anything but pray. The Scriptures do not indicate that they had evangelical intent. They were not holding up signs at the temple entrance saying, "Repent or die." But as they were pursuing God through prayer, they found an opportunity for witness.

Our best opportunities for speaking on his behalf are mostly realized as we walk daily with our Lord in the presence of those around us. Our first and best witness is the life we live. Why? Because when we are seeking God in our daily lives (like the apostles praying at the temple), trusting him by faith through our actions and motives (like the offer of healing for the lame man in the name of Jesus) and watching for opportunities to share what we know (like the attentive crowd that had gathered around), we realize God has provided an audience for us to speak to on his behalf.

What audience has God provided for you? Is it the employees you hire? Is it the other moms at the Tuesday-morning playgroup? Is your audience a classroom of students, a football team or a cheerleading squad? Do you have the ear of your neighbors, your band mates or your hunting buddies? Do you speak regularly with those at your club, in your social group or to someone who makes your coffee every morning? All of us have an audience. We have all been providentially placed for holy conversations, and as we live a life of faith those who are a part of our daily lives naturally provide our best chance to witness.

Point to Life in Jesus

As an audience gathered, Peter seized the opportunity and addressed the people (see Acts 3:12). The word used here is one of several preaching/speaking words the Greek New Testament uses for communication (we'll look at more later). The word *apokrinomai* means to give an answer. It is to speak when something has been said. This implies that questions about the miracle abounded, so Peter simply answered. And his answer was Jesus. Peter steered the focus away from himself and John as miracle workers and pointed to Jesus.

Admittedly, the people had gathered because of the thrill and hype surrounding the healing, but Peter had a different message—the message of resurrection. The healing was only a showcase for the power Jesus Christ displayed in coming back to life. Instead of focusing on the miracle of the lame man walking, Peter focused on the miracle of eternal life for everyone present.

Our message all these years later is still the death, burial and resurrection of Jesus. The reason this remains our message is because it addresses each of our realities. Everyone in our culture is interested in postponing the inevitability of death. We work at preventing death through diet, exercise and medical advances. In our youth, we often ignore death and act like we have plenty of time before it happens to us. But death is a nonrespecter of persons 100 percent of the time. We all die. And since Jesus is the only one who gives us a promise after this inevitability, we always have something to say. We speak of the hope of eternal life that only he can give. The resurrection is the lead message of our witness. Yes, Jesus empowers us. Yes, Jesus heals us. Yes, Jesus walks with us. Yes, Jesus calls us to work in his kingdom. But his victory over our death by victory over his own death is the incredible message we share. Jesus' death, burial and resurrection are the point!

Expect Opposition

Meanwhile, the religious leaders are holding an emergency session of the Sanhedrin (the governing body of the Jewish people in the first century). They have likely gathered at the palatial estate of the high priest, Caiaphas, and they too are talking. According to Acts 4:2, they are "greatly annoyed" at the turn of events. Why are they annoyed? Because this scene is an all-too-familiar flashback to the impromptu teaching sessions that Jesus held in the same temple courts. It was not easy, but they silenced the Jesus movement by crucifying the teacher from Nazareth. But not really. Jesus was no longer around, but his message continued to influence the Jewish populace through the persistent testimony of his followers. So they did what they had authority to do: they shut up the apostles by throwing them in jail.

By the time the entire council had convened, they already knew the details of the story but they still brought Peter and John in for questioning. And those two pressed forward with the same message they had declared to the crowd: Jesus (whom this very council had condemned) had risen from the dead and was the only name given for salvation.

The leaders noted their boldness and commanded Peter and John back to their cell. Then they "conferred" (4:15) among themselves and acknowledged the miracle had taken place (4:16), but instead of believing in Jesus they decided to exert their authority. Thinking that they could silence the apostles, they warned and threatened them, telling them to speak no more in Jesus' name (Acts 4:17, 21). But the warnings and threats didn't work!

Like the apostles, we may face opposition when we speak on Christ's behalf. Increasingly, our culture is opposed to the message of the church. We have earned some of this reaction with dogmatic crusades and judgmental exclusivity, but the fact remains that Jesus is a polarizing figure. Because of this, the world is conferring on how they can stop the message of the gospel. They do it by commanding Christian teachers not to speak of their faith in the classroom. They do it by down-playing the witness portion of a Christian athlete's interview.

They do it by referring to Christmas as the "holiday season." Like the Jewish leaders in the first century, this world knows it can't really deny Christ as a historical figure and the miraculous power often displayed in his church, so they try to quiet the message. In essence, the world's communication to Christ-followers is, "Speak no more of Jesus."

Speak What You Know

Our boldness must mirror that of our first-century brothers. After all the threats, after all the constraints and after all the arrests and time in jail, the response was simple: We cannot *not* speak about what we have seen and heard. Ultimately, Peter and John were obeying God by speaking, but besides that they were eyewitnesses to the events they were talking about. They knew firsthand of the resurrection because they had both been at the empty tomb. They had been there when the Holy Spirit descended on the believers the first day of the church when three thousand were baptized. These men had seen him, eaten with him, talked with him and touched him after his resurrection. They had seen him ascend into heaven with their own eyes. You could threaten all you want, but they knew what they had seen.

That's why the variety of words in this passage used to describe how they spoke are so valuable to us in relation to our own speaking. As mentioned above, Peter and John gave answers to questions, but they also taught (*didaskō*—to give formal instruction) and proclaimed (*katangellō*—to herald) the good news both of the lame man's healing and of Jesus' resurrection.

You and I have not seen many of the things these apostles saw. We did not see Jesus alive after he had died. We were not on the mountain when he floated away in the clouds. And we never saw him walk on water. But we are still witnesses; we have seen and heard. We have seen the hardest of hearts melted by the forgiving love of Jesus. We have seen marriages restored. We have heard prayers that were miraculously answered. And we have seen what God has done in each of our journeys. In other words, when people ask, we can address their questions; when they want to know about our faith, we can instruct them; and while the world is filled with bad news, we can herald the *good* news.

We have seen. We have heard. We speak.

Week One

Devotional Readings

....

MONDAY
A Speaking Compulsion

We cannot but speak of what we have seen and heard.

Some people don't know when to shut up. Their speech is relentless. Their words are endless. Talk. Talk. Talk. Do you know anyone like that?

Years ago, while pastoring a church in Champaign, Illinois, I met one of those incessant gabbers. He could exhaust any blue-ribbon listener. My friend was widely known as someone with a speaking compulsion. Adults avoided him. Children hid from him. It wasn't just his ability to spout off words like an AK-47 on automatic, but it was the fact that he could talk about absolutely nothing in a nonstop, supersonic fashion. The subjects were unlimited. Potholes. Pimples. Rain. Snow. Drought. Green beans. Electricity. Breakfast. Conspiracies. Toothpaste. Toothpicks. Toothaches.

Acts 4:20 is a wonderful reminder that there can be a different kind of speaking compulsion. There can be a divine deliberateness that is marked with immeasurable gratitude and grace. Peter and John, followers of Jesus, were charged not to speak. They were threatened with the promise that if they continued to talk, harm would befall them. Yet they kept on speaking of Jesus. There was no wiggle room in their worldview. They had to talk about him. He was their grand subject. His life was their glorious sermon.

Can that be recovered in us today? It starts with a simple prayer: "Jesus, I put my trust in you. I accept your conditions; by grace through faith I yield my life to you." Watch how he begins to transform you and your words. A speaking compulsion, in the name of Jesus, is birthed.

Because God has spoken, we can speak.

Week One

TUESDAY
When God Speaks

So Abram went, as the LORD had
told him, and Lot went with him.

GENESIS 12:4

As the LORD had told him." Can there possibly be six more
staggering words than those? God spoke. He spoke to a
man. The Creator of heaven and earth communicated. The
Savior and Redeemer of the world talked.

This is the first reference in the Bible to the Hebrew word
dabar. Scripture is loaded with it, occurring some 2,500
times. Generally *dabar* means to speak or talk. Like most
words, its meaning depends on how it is used in a given
context. It is a close cousin to the word ʾamar. "And God said,
'Let there be light'" (Genesis 1:3). ʾAmar, like *dabar,* is a reminder that God is not silent. When God speaks, something
happens. Creation happens! Here in Genesis 12:4, God *told*
Abram what to do, Abram obeyed, and a journey of colossal
faith formation and life transformation was initiated. It
began because God spoke.

I am a father and a grandfather. I cherish those holy moments when my children and grandchildren began to try to
form words. Typically they said things like da-da (daddy),
ma-ma (mommy), wa-wa (water), tank-ou (thank you), peas

(please), bub-buh (brother) or some gibberish that sounded like a word. But they spoke because someone spoke to them first. They imitated their words. That's how it works.

So another pilgrimage of colossal faith formation and genuine life transformation is initiated in us through Christ. God is speaking. Will we speak of him today?

Week One

WEDNESDAY
A Mouth with Company

"Now therefore go, and I will be with your
mouth and teach you what you shall speak."

Exodus 4:12

There is a recurring phrase in Scripture that has fascinated me for some time. Bible students refer to it as the Immanuel Principle. God promises, "I am with you." I have underlined it twenty-one times in my Bible. Other verses hint at God keeping company with us, such as Exodus 29:45 and Leviticus 26:11-12, but the one I've mentioned above will suffice. Notice with me that Exodus 4:12 has a quirky rendition of this Immanuel Principle. Here God promised Moses he would be with his mouth. Strange. Well, perhaps it is not so odd in light of the four excuses that Moses, the reluctant servant leader, offered God: "Who am I?" (3:11); "What shall I say?" (3:13); "They will not believe me" (4:1); and "I am not eloquent" (4:10). This fourth excuse was the essential one in light of Exodus 4:12. Moses hid behind his speech disability.

I understand Moses' hesitation. I stuttered as a kid. A speech therapist came to our home and helped me battle this handicap. If I pause long enough, I can recall the embarrassment I felt in grade school. I can still feel the eyes of my classmates descending upon me as I tried to finish a sentence. I never imagined that God would keep company with my stuttering mouth through almost forty years of ministry. He can do the same for you.

Week One

THURSDAY
A Holy Conversation

> *And when Moses went into the tent of meeting to speak*
> *with the Lord, he heard the voice speaking to him from*
> *above the mercy seat that was on the ark of the testimony,*
> *from between the two cherubim; and it spoke to him.*

NUMBERS 7:89

Twelve days of offerings and celebration concluded the dedication ceremony for the tabernacle of the Lord. That's the context of today's verse. God would now communicate with Moses. Time and time again, God and Moses would enter into a holy conversation. The words *speak, speaking* and *spoke* in this verse are the same Hebrew word we talked about on Tuesday: *dabar.* Throughout the unfolding narrative of God's relationship with Israel, he would repeatedly speak with Moses. In a parallel verse, Exodus 33:11, the Scriptures remind us: "Thus the Lord used to speak to Moses face to face, as a man speaks to his friend." God spoke. Moses listened. Moses spoke. God listened. I love thinking about that exchange. Does God speak in the same way today? I offer a hearty *yes*.

Through the details of his creation, through daily conversations, through his written Word and, more than anything, through the living Word, Jesus, God speaks. This does not require some supernatural avenue. His Word, our Bible, is sufficient. Over and over the Scriptures verify to us that God speaks in and through them. Our holy task is to avoid reading the Word for information only, and instead to read with a desire for the transformation of our heart. This calls for reading it slowly with an active mind, but also with a restful and unhurried heart. When we read it like that a friendship forms, and we can't help but speak to others about him.

Week One

FRIDAY
God's Testimonies, Our Testimony

I will also speak of your testimonies before kings
and shall not be put to shame.

PSALMS 119:46

I f you have walked with Jesus for a while, you have probably heard the term *testimony*. Typically we are encouraged to form, memorize and share with others how we met Jesus. We call that story a *testimony*. In Psalm 119:46, the word is used in a slightly different way. You'll notice that it is in plural form, not singular. The psalmist speaks of God's *testimonies* twenty-three times in this longest chapter of the Bible. *Testimonies* was one of a collection of eight Hebrew words that celebrated God's law. This particular word, *'edah,* is referring to what God declares is his will. This is God's witness of himself. His glory cannot be contained in a single declaration. This psalmist made up his mind that God had spoken. He felt empowered to speak what God had already spoken. He would not hesitate to put his testimony alongside God's *testimonies.* So what?

Our witness to God, what he has done for us in Christ at the cross, does not have to be complicated or dramatic. Sin is sin. All of us are fractured and unable to rescue ourselves. When the reality of that divine rescue fully sets in our heart, we can't help but speak about it. Our gratefulness gives birth to fearlessness.

I once had a much-loved seminary professor describe it in this way: "What God accomplished for us through his son is like putting our finger into an outlet and getting zapped with twenty thousand volts of electricity and surviving." He would chuckle and remind us that we wouldn't simply stand there and never speak of that experience again.

All praise to him. We can speak today.

We Speak Good News

The young married couple smiles at one another knowingly as they enjoy Christmas dinner with the extended family. The conversation sometimes feels slow and awkward to them, but they try to act as normal as possible, making small talk about work, sports, family memories and the weather. Hours later, when the family is gathered around the tree and their parents simultaneously open a box that contains diapers, they are able to share their surprise: "You're going to be grandparents! We're expecting!"

We speak good news.

The high school freshman nervously makes his way down the hallway toward the gym and the coach's office. After two weeks of tryouts, today is the posting of the final team roster. As he turns the corner, the young man spies the list at a distance. It is unceremoniously taped to the block walls with a couple of pieces of athletic tape. At first it is a blur of black letters on a page, but as he gets nearer, it all comes into focus and he sees his name. Hours later, as he rides the bus home, a smile spreads across his face and a deep sense of satisfaction fills his soul. Arriving home, he bursts through the front door, throws his backpack onto the couch and yells, "I made the team!"

We speak good news.

Mom and Dad have been halfheartedly nibbling vending-machine cookies and drinking burnt coffee for the past two hours. Their daughter had fallen out of a tree while playing at a friend's house and suffered serious injuries. She had been conscious but groggy when her parents last saw her being whisked away to surgery. They prayed. They cried. They waited. Eventually the doctor walked in and spoke the words they longed to hear: "Your daughter is going to be fine."

We speak good news.

It was a typical morning cup of coffee at the local big-city Starbucks: sports page, friendly baristas, a Quad Grande Americano and cordial banter between patrons. Then the lead guitarist for the eighties band that had performed the previous night at the arena walked in. Most people were unaware, but an excited fan nearly spilled his coffee trying to get to the cash register to buy this rock legend a cup of joe. The entire conversation was "Hey, let me buy a childhood hero coffee this morning . . . I'm a big fan," followed by "That's cool. Thanks, man." No autographs. No musical discussion. No selfie. Not even a handshake. But for the rest of the day, every conversation began with "Guess who I met at Starbucks this morning."

We speak good news.

It is human to do so. When something happens that brings us joy and may bring joy into the lives of those we know, we naturally share it with them. There is no training needed for this. There are no "good news teller" qualifications. It's not that hard. It's reflexive. You just open your mouth and excitedly tell what you know. "I'm engaged." "I got the promotion." "We won." "I'm cancer-free." And just like that, good news has been spoken.

It seems easy, doesn't it? Yet, for some reason, this human tendency to share good news gets complicated when it comes to talking about the good news we have in Jesus. Somehow Christ-followers can share good news about almost everything in their lives, but they struggle sharing the best news concerning their salvation. Why? Well, throughout the years, I've encountered three primary reasons for our silence when it comes to sharing the good news of the kingdom.

1. Christians feel unqualified to share news that is so good. (*What if they ask me questions about God I can't answer?*)

2. Christians are afraid that others won't believe the good news when it is shared. (*What if they don't believe me?*)

3. Christians don't understand the urgency of the situation. (*Someday I'll share Jesus with my friends. I'm just waiting for the right time.*)

While all of these seem to be plausible reasons for our silence, they don't hold up under the light. Maybe a story from the Old Testament will help us understand why we must let go of these untruths.

First the Bad News

Good news often comes as a response to bad news, and the news we find in 2 Kings 6–7 is bad. At that time in history, the Northern Kingdom of Israel (born out of rebellion against God) had continued in its evil ways under the reign of its current king, Joram. Because of this, the pattern of sin-warning-punishment-repentance-sin continued throughout the history of this faction of God's people.

When we are transported through the biblical narrative to the capital city of Samaria, we find it in full punishment mode. Ben-hadad, the king from Syria to the north, had laid siege against the city (2 Kings 6:24). This was an ancient war technique in which an army shut up all routes in and out of a city with the goal of starving those trapped within to surrender.

The siege was working. The people inside Samaria were experiencing a shortage of food that caused them to seek nourishment in some unthinkable ways. It appears that donkey heads had become a part of the menu. "There was a great famine in Samaria, as they besieged it, until a donkey's head was sold for eighty shekels of silver" (2 Kings 6:25). This shows the extent of their hunger; the donkey was considered an unclean animal, and its head renders little meat. But the hunger was even more severe than this. Though animal dung was commonly used for fuel in Bible times, this story may indicate that dove's dung was actually being eaten. Worse yet, there is the story of two women deciding to eat their infant children. (See 2 Kings 6:28-29 for details.) The point is that these people were hungry in a way that most of us could never imagine.

Along with this came the daily realization that they were not free to come and go as they pleased. From within the walled city situated on the hill, they could see the smoke of the enemy's campfires rising up all around them. Sentries on the wall regularly updated the people as to the activities of the Syrian army. Through cracks in the wooden gate, they could see their homes and farms on the surrounding plain. And all around, people carried desperate looks of hunger, despair, pain and fear.

There is nothing quite like being in a bad situation in which there seems no way out. And that's exactly what these Israelites were experiencing. There was no escape. But, as the saying goes, "Someone always has it worse off than you." And in this case, those worse off were four lepers that sat at the town gate.

It's very likely, given the detestable disease of these four men, that their place at the gate was outside the wall and not inside it. Their exact location at the gate cannot be determined biblically, but we do know that these men at the gate of a city were starving and under siege. As beggars, their survival was normally dependent on alms given by generous citizens, but due to the siege and subsequent famine, the people they normally counted on for daily provisions had nothing to give. They were obviously doomed to starve to death.

And so they reasoned together that since they were going to die anyway, why not take matters into their own hands. "Now come, let's go over to the camp of the Syrians. If they spare our lives we shall live, and if they kill us we shall but die" (2 Kings 7:4). As evening descended on the plain surrounding Samaria, these four unnamed men made their way down the road that led into the enemy's camp. Soon they would know their fate.

Now for the Good News

What they had no way of knowing was that God had gone before them. The chronicler of the king's history reveals what these lepers had no foreknowledge of. The Lord caused the Syrians to hear the sound of an approaching army, and they fled in absolute panic. They left everything and ran for their lives. They left their campfires burning. They left their combat sandals at the entrance to their tents. They left their wineskins, their crusty bread and their stores of food. In an inexplicable move, given the distance to their home country, they even left their horses!

Enter the four lepers.

To their great amazement and joy, and unbeknownst to the people back in town, the famine and imprisonment were over. In their exuberance, the lepers proceeded to the first tent, where they gorged themselves on dried fish, cheese and sweet dates. They lifted wineskins to their lips and guzzled until the red juice dripped down their beards. It had been weeks since they had even seen such food, let alone eaten any. They feasted, stopping only long enough to grab some money and clothes, and quickly hid them for future use. Even then, their hunger persisted so they returned to the camp for more free food and clothing.

Finally, their appetites satisfied and their futures secured, they realized the enormity of the situation. The terrible siege was no longer a reality, and the devastating hunger was no longer necessary. The army had fled. There was plenty of food for everyone in Samaria. And they were convicted. "Then they said to one another, 'We are not doing right. This day is a day of good news. If we are silent and wait until the morning light, punishment will overtake us. Now therefore come; let us go and tell the king's household'" (2 Kings 7:9).

Unlikely Spokesmen

So, with an awareness of the magnitude of their news and the determination to share it, these four men made their way back up the road leading to the main gate of Samaria. And yet, an obstacle remained—one we mentioned earlier that affects those who would share good news. What qualified these guys to be the bearers of good news? And why would anyone listen to them? These men were undeniably unlikely spokesmen.

In ancient times, lepers lived at the bottom of the social ladder. Due to their very visible skin disease, they were banned from all public gatherings. According to the law, they had to make a loud declaration of "unclean" anytime someone came into their presence. Their sores were painful. Their looks were deplorable. Their shame was visible. Only their hunger for human touch matched their appetite for bread. And they were the butt of jokes, enduring stares of disgust while noticing the effort others made to avoid eye contact.

It is no surprise, then, that when these untouchables shouted their news to the soldier on the wall in the final watch of the night, their message was met with skepticism. The sentry may have blurted out, "The Syrian army has left their camp? Yeah, right!" But the prospect that the camp may indeed be empty was worth waking the king as the first light of dawn chased the shadows of the palace away.

Of course, the king didn't believe them either. He was convinced that this was some sort of trap, but after a small reconnaissance party confirmed the story of the lepers, he ordered that the gates be opened. The people flooded out of the city as the sun rose, and they plundered the Syrian camp.

We never hear of those four unnamed men again. But we know that they changed the reality of an entire city. The starving people of Samaria felt the satisfaction of nourishment and the trapped people of Samaria felt freedom once again. All because four men decided to speak good news.

As followers of Jesus, we are called to share good news. Jesus came declaring, "I must preach the good news of the kingdom of God to the other towns as well; for I was sent for this purpose" (Luke 4:43). He sent his initial followers to do the same—declaring that the kingdom of God was at hand. In the early church, the evangelist Philip "preached the good news about the kingdom of God and the name of Jesus Christ" (Acts 8:12). And from that time until the present, "good news" is the best description of our Christian message.

And though we are separated by centuries of history and thousands of miles geographically, the news hasn't changed much. Like these Bible characters long ago, we have discovered through the miraculous provision of God some really good news. And, amazingly, the good news the lepers found in the empty Syrian camp strongly resembles the good news we have found in Jesus Christ. The desperation of those around us is the same, and the possibilities are just as joyous and life giving.

We speak the good news of nourishment to those who are starving. There is a deep hunger in our culture for love, relationship, belonging and purpose. A famine of true companionship is evidenced by the rise in dating services and social media. There is a strong desire to find a person to love and to collect "friends" and "followers" from all over the world. And a young generation searches for worth expressed through various forms of sexual expression. It's like this world has a spiritual diet that includes donkey heads . . . and worse.

Only Jesus can satisfy the deep hunger within each of us. After meeting the physical needs of thousands, feeding them all with a couple of fish and five loaves, Jesus said to them, "I am the bread of life; whoever comes to me shall not hunger, and whoever believes in me shall never thirst'" (John 6:35). There is good news for our friends, neighbors, coworkers and fellow students who are trying to fill up on the world's fare but who remain unsatisfied. If we can learn to categorize everyone's life pursuits as spiritual hunger, then talking about Jesus is simply sharing the good news that their spiritual famine is over.

We also speak good news of freedom for those who are enslaved. Those who sin are slaves to sin. In his writing to the Roman Christians, the apostle Paul points out that death to the old self through Jesus' death means "that we would no longer be enslaved to sin" (Romans 6:6). And then he claims, "you have been set free from sin" (6:22). Think of the spiritual and emotional bondage those around us experience every day: those addicted to the numbing effect of drugs and alcohol; those caught in the pattern of sexual addiction; those who can't get past the pain of their past; those who are disgusted with themselves and are sure God can't love them; those who are depressed and feel no worth; those who have been abused in a variety of ways; those who lie to and hide from others. These kinds of sin are nothing more than imprisonment. It's not unlike being trapped in the filth, desperation and disgust behind the walls of Samaria.

But there is a way out. Jesus can free all the trapped people in our lives from their sin and the pain inevitably attached to it. Romans 8:1-2 says, "There is therefore now no condemnation for those who are in Christ Jesus. For the law of the Spirit of life has set you free in Christ Jesus from the law of sin and death." Instead of looking down on others for the sin that entangles them, maybe we can find the courage to speak by offering them freedom in Christ. We speak of Jesus. We are sharing the good news that they don't have to stay in their sin. Through Christ they are free to leave it behind and truly live.

So we offer spiritual food for the spiritually starved and spiritual freedom for the spiritually trapped. But, once again, why us?

Like the lepers, we may be woefully unworthy as spokes-
persons for God, but we are qualified simply because of what
we know. We have found nourishment and freedom in Christ.
We speak good news because we have experienced it.

Like the lepers, we may fear that no one will believe our
story, but someone not believing in the good news does not
negate its truth. Jesus really can change lives, because he
really has changed ours. We speak good news because we
know its truth.

Like the lepers, we may focus on how our needs have been
met, but sooner or later we're going to be convicted that time
is of the essence for those who don't have what we do. People
need Jesus now. We speak good news because today (today!)
is a day of good news, but we are keeping it to ourselves.

Week Two

Devotional Readings

....

MONDAY
Saved People Speak Up

> *Then they said to one another, "We are not doing right. This day is a day of good news. If we are silent and wait until the morning light, punishment will overtake us. Now therefore come; let us go and tell the king's household."*

2 KINGS 7:9

Few people can keep good news a secret. Think back to the different scenarios described in the introduction to chapter two: a young couple is expecting a baby, a high school freshman makes the team, a mom and dad receive the news that their daughter is going to be fine, and someone encounters a rock star at a local Starbucks. Could any of us resist the urge to speak up in any one of those scenarios? Almost all of us, like the lepers in 2 Kings 7, are compelled to share what we have experienced. The rest of this week we will devote our attention to looking at leper stories in the New Testament. In every circumstance, there is an irresistible compulsion to speak up. That's what people do who have encountered Jesus and have been saved.

I was seven years old or so and had not yet taken swimming lessons. My parents warned me of getting too close to the water's edge. It had stormed the previous night, and I couldn't resist the temptation to throw small branches into the lake. Of course, I got too close, fell in, sank to the bottom and had to be rescued. I've never forgotten. Decades have come and gone, but I can still recall the vivid details of being saved. How much more, then, should my saving encounter with Jesus prompt me to speak up? Saved people speak up. Amen and amen.

Week Two

TUESDAY
That Irresistible Urge to Speak Up

> And a leper came to [Jesus] . . . and kneeling said to him,
> "If you will, you can make me clean." Moved with pity, he
> stretched out his hand and touched him. . . . And Jesus . . .
> said to him, "See that you say nothing to anyone. . . . " But
> he went out and began to talk freely about it, and to
> spread the news, so that Jesus could no longer openly
> enter a town.
>
> MARK 1:40-41, 43-45

Here is one of life's great ironies. Jesus instructed a restored leper not to talk about his healing until he had gone to the priest and fulfilled the law's demand (see Leviticus 13–14). Instead this leper began to talk freely about what Jesus had done for him. And because of that irresistible urge to speak up, Jesus was unable to enter a town without creating a mob scene.

It would be easy for us to criticize this well-intentioned leper. After all, his talking brought a halt to Jesus' healing ministry in that area of Galilee. But isn't that the nature of someone who has been marginalized by society and then restored? This leper can't help himself. As already mentioned, lepers were excluded from the rhythms of everyday life. The one time they were instructed to speak up was when they entered a village or town, and on that occasion their words were to bring attention to themselves and their disease. They were commanded to shout, "Unclean, unclean!" (Leviticus 13:45). Jesus changed all of that. He touched this man, making himself unclean, so that the leper could become clean.

Don't miss it. Isn't that the nature of God? He takes a sin-riddled self and exchanges it for a Savior-filled purpose. When that exchange is truly grasped, who could resist speaking up for Jesus?

Week Two

WEDNESDAY
Why I Speak Up

In that hour he healed many people of diseases and plagues and evil spirits, and on many who were blind he bestowed sight. And he answered them, "Go and tell John what you have seen and heard: the blind receive their sight, the lame walk, lepers are cleansed, and the deaf hear, the dead are raised up, the poor have good news preached to them. And blessed is the one who is not offended by me."

LUKE 7:21-23

As strange as it sounds, John the Baptist was vacillating. That's why Jesus spoke these words in Luke 7. John had been arrested and imprisoned by Herod and now needed some reassurance that Jesus was the promised Messiah. Notice with me all the evidences of good news: the blind see, the lame walk, the lepers are cleansed, the deaf hear, the dead are raised, and the poor have the gospel preached to them. Whoever these disciples of John were, Jesus instructed them to "go and tell" their mentor that Jesus fulfilled all the messianic promises found in places like Isaiah 61. Doubt can come to all of us. Jesus alone can drive it away.

I went through a dark night of the soul during which I questioned the love of God. I wondered if he really cared and had crafted a meaningful purpose for my life. I know that kind of struggle can sound scandalous to some. And that's the exact word Jesus used in Luke 7:23: "Blessed is the one who is not offended [or scandalized] by me." Prison and experiences of the dark night can erode faith. Jesus reminded John and us that good news is for those who depend solely on him. I speak up because I have found Jesus to be true.

Week Two

THURSDAY
Guess Who Came to Dinner

And while he [Jesus] was at Bethany in the house of Simon
the leper, as he was reclining at table, a woman came with
an alabaster flask of ointment of pure nard, very costly,
and she broke the flask and poured it over his head.

MARK 14:3

Almost all commentaries focus on the unnamed woman who came with an alabaster flask of expensive nard. Perhaps rightly so. John, in his account, tells us it was Mary, sister of Lazarus and Martha (John 12:2-8) who performed this selfless act. After all, Mary was preparing Jesus for the cross because of her devotion to him (Luke 10:39). However, this mealtime scene is disturbingly abrupt when it reveals that the host was Simon the leper, who is mentioned only in connection with this story.

John implies that Martha catered the meal. Who else would do it? Her reputation for cooking blue-ribbon meals was well-known. But what do we do with Simon the leper? We don't know much about him. Maybe Jesus had healed him and out of deep gratitude he invited Jesus to a meal. Maybe he was a bachelor and a lousy cook, but a friend of Martha's and knew she could save the day. Maybe he was still suffering from leprosy but knew the nature of Jesus, and threw caution to the wind by inviting the one person to dinner who could save him from all of his heartache. Who knows? The one obvious fact is that his disease stuck to his name: "Simon the leper." Truth be told, I am "J. K. the sinner."

Can you imagine Simon not speaking up about this defining day? Never. And so it should be with you and me. We are all sinners saved by grace.

Week Two

FRIDAY
One Loud Voice

And as he entered a village, he was met by ten lepers, who stood at a distance and lifted up their voices, saying, "Jesus, Master, have mercy on us." When he saw them he said to them, "Go and show yourselves to the priests." And as they went they were cleansed. Then one of them, when he saw that he was healed, turned back, praising God with a loud voice. . . . Now he was a Samaritan.

LUKE 17:12-16

We started the week with four lepers shouting good news at the gate of Samaria (2 Kings 7:10), and we end the week with one leper shouting good news somewhere in a village on the border of Samaria and Galilee (Luke 17:15). Talk about coming full circle. I love the symmetry of Scripture. And I love the enormous fact that people who have experienced a life change tend to speak up.

The irony in this passage is that only one of the original ten lepers returned to do that very thing. Only one gave Jesus thanks. Amazingly, this man was not only ostracized because of his disease, but also marginalized because he was a Samaritan. Perhaps that is exactly what it takes: to realize the immensity of our healing and the enormity of our journey in order to be witnesses of our salvation by Jesus.

Some people are wired with a loud voice. Who hasn't sat in a restaurant attempting to enjoy a quiet meal with that special person we love, only to be interrupted and irritated by the obnoxious voice of someone at the adjacent table? I'm an introvert by personality, but I assure you that given the right subject, in the right moment, I can be as loud as that person who has forgotten his indoor voice.

At the cross, Jesus Christ did for me what I could not do for myself. He took away my sin. He gave me new life. He restored my joy. I now have a purpose-filled life. I return to Jesus regularly and often and thank him for what he did. More than that, I am growing in my desire, even at sixty-two years old, to speak up with a loud voice of my colossal love for him. We speak good news because what Jesus did for us can't help but be told.

three

We Speak Even If
No One Listens

The Bible was opened to the texts of both Psalm 23 and John 11. The preacher had written notes to speak words of encouragement based on life found only in Christ and the hope of the resurrection. The fifteen-minute sermon was delivered with great passion, and the truth was boldly spoken. The organ music was slow but meditative, and the sweet smell of floral arrangements filled the room. And yet it can confidently be said that no one listened to the sermon that day. How do I know? Well, because I was the one who preached it, and the circumstances surrounding the occasion for it dictated that it be preached but not heard.

I was a twenty-four-year-old youth minister in Kissimmee, Florida, when I performed my very first funeral. I had not been the first choice. The funeral home had asked for every other pastor on our staff, but none were available, so I said yes. Then I learned that my first funeral would likely end up being the most unique one I would ever do. A ninety-seven-year-old woman who had spent her entire life in Kissimmee had passed away. She was an only child who never married and had outlived all of her family and friends. Because she lived a life of seclusion for many years, she had no acquaintances. But she did have a will, and that will stipulated a funeral service upon her death. This is where I came in.

When I arrived at the funeral home, the director spoke in that typical low and hushed voice while giving me instructions concerning the woman's ceremony. *Surely, someone will show up for this woman's funeral,* I thought as I sat in a chair in front of the closed casket. But no one came. The music faded, and I stood to face an empty room of chairs. I read Psalm 23. I prayed. I read her obituary. And then I preached a sermon about Jesus being the resurrection and the life from John 11. And no one listened.

Ezekiel Speaks

As unusual as this situation was it certainly took the pressure off an inexperienced preacher, and it was nothing compared to the challenge the Old Testament prophet Ezekiel faced, as recorded in the book bearing his name. He was not sent to an empty funeral home, but to the Jewish exiles to warn them of the impending consequences of their disobedience. But he was warned that they probably wouldn't listen. We read that God commanded him to "speak my words to them, whether they hear or refuse to hear" (Ezekiel 2:7). The prophet's calling and the implications behind it will be the focus of this chapter, but first it will be helpful to get our historical bearings.

We can deduce from the book itself that Ezekiel is its author because he writes in first person, "I saw visions of God," as he gives us his identity: "the word of the LORD came to Ezekiel" (1:1, 3). He also gives us a valuable time reference and location clues stating that these visions came "as I was among the exiles by the Chebar canal" and "it was the fifth year of the exile of King Jehoiachin" (1:2). This means that we can reasonably associate Ezekiel with a group of nobility that was taken captive by King Nebuchadnezzar during the reign of Jehoiachin around 599 B.C. So the fifth year of this king's captivity finds Ezekiel the priest living in some sort of Jewish settlement in Babylon around 594 B.C. (see 2 Kings 24:10-17). This becomes his place of ministry for the next twenty-five years. And though he spoke throughout this time, there were no immediate results from his message.

This is not what most people (including prophets) expect when they dare to communicate God's Word and truth to others. Preachers and prophets alike are hopeful that people will repent of their sins, change their ways or be inspired to greater spirituality as a result of their words. Most don't expect a Billy Graham Crusade type of response at the invitation, but an occasional "Amen!" would be encouraging. Unfortunately, it often feels like there is no real life change as a result of the teaching.

This result is not relegated to vocational speakers like preachers and prophets. Just about any Christ-follower who earnestly prays for the lost and shares the gospel message anticipates some sort of spiritual result (such as a person becoming a Christian as a result of the message that we share). Yet, like Ezekiel, we often speak with no visible results.

Another thing in the Ezekiel story mirrors some of the obstacles we face as we share the good news. God compelled him to speak through visuals and visions that were strange and mysterious. Unlike Jonah, who simply went to Nineveh with his one-line sermon, "Yet forty days, and Nineveh shall be overthrown" (Jonah 3:4), Ezekiel not only prophesied but also became a human object lesson of communication for God and a revealer of some pretty weird dreams.

For example, in Ezekiel 4, God told Ezekiel to make a model of Jerusalem under siege. So he made a miniature version of the holy city, including battering rams, siege walls and presumably tiny men and horses. He must have looked like a kid playing with action figures. And as if this weren't enough, he was then told to lie on his side for over a year with an iron skillet separating his face from the miniature city. This was to illustrate God's message that he would turn his face from the unrepentant house of Judah. Can you imagine how humiliated this preacher must have felt? I can hear parents' warnings: "Kids, stay away from that Ezekiel guy—he's crazy." Visuals like this were a part of his entire career.

Not only did he act out God's judgment in some very peculiar ways, but he also received some visions that set off weirdo alarms. He told a parable of two eagles and a vine in chapter 17 and envisioned a valley of dry bones in chapter 37. Add to this some sermons addressed directly to mountains, and you've got one eccentric spokesperson for God.

The truth is that every messenger for God faces some environmental and speaking challenges. A few years ago, a friend of mine in California related to me his church's problem in relation to the upcoming state vote concerning a gay marriage bill. The problem was not what they believed about homosexuality but the way most conversations with non-Christians began. Before they could even begin to share the good news of Christ, they were asked, "What is your church's stance on the proposed bill?" The answer often shut the ears, hearts and minds of the would-be believer before these Christians could invite them to church.

They were shut out before a word was spoken. The hindrances to your message may not be as obvious, but chances are you will face obstacles to your witness from time to time.

Consider the challenges you may be facing as you speak for God. Maybe your supervisor at work is suggesting that the Bible study you lead at lunchtime is "forcing your religion on others." Maybe it's undue pressure at work from an atheist supervisor to keep your religion to yourself. Maybe it's being shunned by coworkers because they know of your convictions. Sometimes by avoiding conversation with us, even family and close friends do not allow us to speak into their lives. Maybe it is a rough ministry location that is virtually opposed to Christianity. Maybe it is the moral failure of a well-known Christian that causes the message to fall on deaf ears. Many situations can hinder our message, and many people will never listen to what we have to say, but still we speak.

Why would anyone continue to speak for God when there is obviously no positive response to the message spoken? Why did Ezekiel keep speaking words of prophecy, and why do we keep speaking the truth of the gospel when it seems that there are no results. Truthfully, it's not easy, but what we know about the God we speak for and what we know about ourselves and those we speak to compel us to keep talking.

What Every Speaker for God Must Know

To begin with, we speak because of who God is and his relationship to us. He says to his prophet, "Son of man, stand on your feet, and I will speak with you" (Ezekiel 2:1). Our God is a God of communication. He starts the conversation with us. Our speaking begins and ends with him.

Our calling is from God. He says to Ezekiel, "Son of man,

I send you to the people of Israel" and again "I send you to them" (2:3, 4). We speak because God has sent us to speak. He could have come up with many communication plans, but the one he settled on was to use those who have received the good news of Jesus to spread that good news. This is why we refer to Jesus' farewell speech in Matthew 28 as the Great Commission. He sends his followers by saying, "Go," and what he sends us to do is to speak of his mission, his teaching, his baptism and his kingdom (see Matthew 28:19-20). We speak on his authority and because he has told us to speak.

Our message is from God. Again, God's calling to Ezekiel reminds us of our own "you shall say to them, 'Thus says the Lord GOD'" (2:4) and "you shall speak my words to them" (2:7). When we speak on God's behalf, the words are not our own. When we speak of becoming a new creation in Christ, we're only repeating God's creative words "let there be light" (Genesis 1:3). When we share the message of Jesus as the Savior of the world, we are simply articulating the living Word of God. When we preach, teach, share or explain the Bible, we are only repeating the written Word of God that has been around for millennia.

This is a crucial thing to remember for those of us who speak on God's behalf: these are not our words. We didn't create them. We don't have to back them up. We don't have to accomplish them. We don't have to defend them. We are truly reading the script of love that God wrote for this world long before there was a world. Seriously, don't put the pressure of the message on yourself. It's not our message; we speak God's word.

People are people. Now that we have the message, what do we need to know about the people we are preaching to?

More than anyone, God understands the tendency of human-kind to shut our ears. Since Adam and Eve rejected eternal communion with God in the garden by rebelling with the forbidden fruit, God has been speaking and humans have been stopping their ears. Before Ezekiel speaks a word for him, God reminds him of the challenges that he will face with people. Here's what he says about the people of Israel:

- They are "nations of rebels, who have rebelled against me" (2:3).
- "They and their fathers have transgressed against me" (2:3).
- "Their descendants are also impudent and stubborn" (2:4).
- They are a "rebellious house" (three times: 2:5, 6, 7).

In describing the people of Israel, God has also described the people we go to school with, the people we play sports with, the people we hang out with, the people we live with, the people we go to church with and, yes, the person we look at in the mirror each day. These are the very people we hope to reach with our message. The ones we speak to have a history of being the kind of people who don't listen. This can be a challenge for those of us who want results from our speaking, because the human condition—both biblically and culturally—dictates that our witnessing efforts are often two steps forward and one step back.

Thankfully God has made a way to redeem our human condition of sin. He has provided a way to forgive us through Jesus and to convict us, change us and grow us by his Spirit. Our audience may be difficult, but understanding that they (which is to say "we") have rebelled against God may comfort us when we feel like they have rejected us. It also enhances the message of redemption. For just as God pursued the rebellious house of Israel in Ezekiel's time, he pursues a world of rebels today. And he has provided a way to come to him through his Son. In a strange way, the rebelliousness of our audience enhances the message we have. God pursuing humanity is news. God pursuing constantly rebellious humanity is *good* news.

What everyone who hears our message must know. If we could travel back in time toward the end of Ezekiel's life and interview those nonrepentant, nonlistening, hard-headed Israelites, I wonder what they would say if we asked them about Ezekiel. Some may say, "He was crazy" or "He was too negative—always prophesying doom" or "His preaching style was unorthodox." But I bet if we pressed hard enough, many would admit that they believed he truly had a relationship with God and that they admired his courage. This may be enough for those of us who speak today as well. Maybe what they know about the messenger is part of the communication.

A prophet has been among them. Ezekiel was called to be a prophet. God said that the people will know that a prophet has been among them. The Hebrew word for "prophet" is *navi'*. Generally speaking, it means to speak a word from God, but we find a rich layer to this word when we consider it comes from a root that may mean "to cause to bubble up, hence to pour forth words abundantly"[1] like this picture of what it means to speak the word of God. The words of a prophet bubble up from deep within and overflow with the life-giving and refreshing Word of the living God. And those who encounter this messenger know it.

I believe this is the kind of refreshment that causes those around us to know there is something different about us and the words we speak. Because of the Spirit's presence in our lives, they know down deep that our relationship with God is authentic. Our friends may not respond to our invitation to come to church with them, but they sense the faith that causes us to ask. Our coworkers may tire of our churchy language and visible faith, but when crisis hits, they know where to turn for prayer. Our neighbors may associate us with many misconceptions concerning Christianity in our culture, but they also observe how loving, accepting and caring we seem to be. The citizens of the small town may never frequent the doors of the steepled white church building, but they know that the preacher is speaking the word of God every Sunday. In other words, when we speak, we represent the presence of God to those around us. Those who hear our words know there is a bubbling fountain of truth they can turn to at any time they wish.

We are not afraid. They also may notice something else. During his calling, God specifically encourages Ezekiel not to be afraid. "And you, son of man, be not afraid of them, nor be afraid of their words. . . . Be not afraid of their words, nor be dismayed at their looks" (2:6). Why did he tell him not to be afraid? Because fear is a great hindrance to speaking on God's behalf. Over the years, I have heard at least two recurring fears that most people experience when it comes to sharing their faith. One is that they won't be able to answer all the questions someone may pose about Christianity. But the greatest fear is that their message will be rejected.

At the church where I serve, we use the phrase "dangerous witness" to describe the kind of speakers we want to become for God. The idea of "dangerous witness" comes from the Greek word *martyreō*, which means to "testify" or "witness." This is where we get our word *martyr*, which means to die for one's faith. Historically speaking, millions have been martyred for speaking on Jesus' behalf, yet persecution always seems to embolden Christians. This hasn't always resulted in more conversions, but in an underlying respect that seems to accompany the courage to speak. Again, not much has changed since the time and ministry of Ezekiel when it comes to speaking for God. We may be tempted to be afraid of people who don't listen to our message, oppose our message with harsh and threatening words or mock our message with the faces they make, but still God calls us not to fear.

Sometimes we speak and no one listens. But keep speaking because the God who fulfilled every word he spoke through Ezekiel is the same God who will do the same with us. And sometimes that is enough.

Week Three

Devotional Readings

....

MONDAY
We Speak Even When No One Listens

> *And you shall speak my words to them, whether they hear or refuse to hear, for they are a rebellious house.*
>
> EZEKIEL 2:7

I f you have ever coached athletes, taught students, raised kids or led a team, you know what it is like to speak and have no one pay attention to your words. Many of us have experienced that intense frustration, and that's the plight of the prophet Ezekiel. He was probably from an aristocratic family and certainly a part of the temple priesthood (1:3). Somewhere around 599 to 597 B.C. he and others were exiled to Babylon where he faithfully served for the next quarter century.

With orders in hand, Ezekiel daily poured out his heart to his fellow exiles and those left behind in Jerusalem, calling them to repentance. He became a living illustration, a flesh-and-blood PowerPoint slide of God's warning and judgment.

God reminded the prophet to speak his words and nothing but his words. Ezekiel's divine assignment was clear: speak even when no one listens.

Please don't miss the irony implied in today's verse. Ezekiel was called and commissioned to be God's spokesman. So are we.

There is a great deal of conjecture about what *navi'*, the Hebrew term for "prophet," actually means. On one level it describes someone whose job was "to announce" or "to proclaim" what God had already said in the law. Prophets were covenant cops. *Navi'* describes someone who is literally "bubbling over" or "pouring out" a God-prompted message. Ezekiel is a vivid reminder that we are commissioned to speak even when no one listens because we have a burden for lost people.

Week Three

TUESDAY
We Speak Even When It Doesn't Make Sense

*And whether they hear or refuse to hear (for they
are a rebellious house) they will know that a
prophet has been among them.*

EZEKIEL 2:5

Perhaps you noticed that we took two steps back in se-
lecting the devotional passage today. Yesterday we read
2:7 and today we read 2:5. Our text reminds us that sometimes God's commission is confusing, or at least it feels that
way. If we could take the time to locate all the specific references to what this calling of God meant for Ezekiel, we would
discover some incredibly strange experiences. He was called
to eat a scroll, crawl through a hole in the temple wall, fashion
a model city of Jerusalem on a brick, build a siege against it,
shave himself with a sword and divide the hair, lie on his left
side for 390 days, lie on his right side for forty days, cook
with cow dung, not mourn the passing of his own wife,
prophesy to mountains, preach to dead and dry bones, and
on and on.

Ezekiel's name actually means "God strengthens." How ap-
propriate. It is hugely important that I remind all of us, including
me, that being a Jesus-follower gives us no guarantee that we

will always understand the prompting voice of God. This very day he could call us to speak of Jesus to our resistant neighbor. This very day he might orchestrate a divine appointment of sharing good news with a total stranger at our local Walmart. This very day he may very well direct us to that hardened family member who has rejected Jesus and his church again and again. These things happen; I can testify to God's strange ways. We speak even when it doesn't make sense. Stay alert.

Week Three

WEDNESDAY
We Speak Even When No One Else Does

And I sought for a man among them who should build up
the wall and stand in the breach before me for the land,
that I should not destroy it, but I found none.

EZEKIEL 22:30

I have been drawn to this verse for years. I first memorized it back in 1974 while standing post, serving our country in that faraway place called Germany. I was drawn to God's intense search for a "breach man" (or a "breach woman"), someone he could use to his glory. God was, according to this verse, specifically looking for someone who could lead his people to repentance, someone who would call Israel back to the original covenant. I was reminded, all those years ago, that only Jesus ultimately and finally has the perfect character to stand in the gap and be the breach man between God and us. Praise his name! That truth, however, does not diminish our usefulness for God's glory. When I read the story of this prophet, it appears that he stood alone. But Ezekiel served God's purpose alongside other fearless spokesmen, such as Daniel, Shadrach, Meshach and Abednego.

God continues to search for ready and useful people. Perhaps you are the only disciple in your family who has come to faith in Jesus. Maybe you are the only Jesus-follower that you know of in your workplace. It might be that no student in your school except you has openly identified as an apprentice to Jesus. I would remind you of a simple but essential truth: there are breach men and women, imperfect though they be, ready to speak even when no one else does. How about you?

Week Three

THURSDAY
We Speak Even When
the Message Seems Small

> *Say to them, As I live, declares the Lord God, I have no*
> *pleasure in the death of the wicked, but that the wicked*
> *turn from his way and live; turn back, turn back from*
> *your evil ways, for why will you die, O house of Israel?*

Ezekiel 33:11

I readily understand how difficult passages like this one can be to read. It doesn't sound like an ounce of good news exists here. Put yourself in Israel's place. Ezekiel's prophecy rings of hopelessness. Sin and rebellion had completely marred God's relationship with his people. Did a two-word sermon "Turn back" make any difference in 599 B.C.? Can a message of turning back to God, as Creator and Savior, make a speck of difference in today's world? It seems so . . . small.

Truth be told, sometimes it feels as if the church is losing ground. The enemy, Satan, and his forces run roughshod over marriages and families. So many universities continue to march toward a godless social agenda. Christians around the world are persecuted. Wars and rumors of war, disease, earthquakes, floods, man's inhumanity to man, continual injustice, hatred and all sorts of other demonic activities give some credence to hopelessness. But then—and with God, there is always a "but then"—he reminds us that he finds no pleasure in the death of the wicked.

I can't read this passage and not hear 2 Peter 3:9: "The Lord is not slow to fulfill his promise as some count slowness, but is patient toward you, not wishing that any should perish, but that all should reach repentance." God is at work. He invites us to stand next to him. With love and grace, we speak, "Turn back, turn back." In Jesus' name, amen.

Week Three

FRIDAY
We Speak Even When It Seems Impossible

*So I prophesied as I was commanded. And as I prophesied,
there was a sound, and behold, a rattling, and the
bones came together, bone to its bone.*

EZEKIEL 37:7

Ezekiel must have lost his prophetic robe and turban when those dry bones put on flesh and came alive. For my money, this is one of the most remarkable stories told in the entire metanarrative of Scripture. These bones represented the whole dried-up, hopeless and cut-off house of Israel (37:11). Talk about impossible. Yet if God could bring an entire valley of dry bones to life, was there anything he could not do? So Ezekiel prophesied and God did the resurrecting. It must have been a sight! Call it whatever you want: restoration, reconciliation or revival. Ezekiel did what he was asked to do and God did the rest.

I knew a man who dabbled with religion. He was fiercely independent, so any talk of submission to Jesus fell on deaf ears. He had a Grand Canyon–sized hole in his heart, having been wounded in a dysfunctional home, embittered by an abusive father, angry at the world, ashamed of his own cowardly behavior and incapable of putting his life back together. He drank in order to quiet his soul's pleading. He ran from relationships that became too intimate, afraid of being discovered.

Then, on an early-spring morning, he encountered a man who knew Jesus—really knew Jesus. That disciple shared the good news, and this broken man met his Savior and entered into a relationship that changed everything.

Perhaps you've guessed by now that the fractured religious man was me. I was a walking set of dry bones, but an Ezekiel-like servant of God dared to speak, and the impossible became possible. So, we speak.

four

We Speak Powerfully
in Weakness

Dave Busby was a powerful youth speaker. At Christian youth conventions and conferences all over the country, he held the attention of students from every background and spiritual level in a unique way. It was as if they were hanging on every word as this man passionately poured out his heart about Jesus. He could make them laugh and cry, but mostly he inspired teenagers to live their lives for Christ instead of for themselves. When he finished speaking and offered an invitation, hundreds would pour out of their seats, into the aisles and to the front of the stage to make decisions for Jesus. Dynamic. Influential. Popular. Inspirational. Passionate. Spirit-filled. All of these and more are words that describe his preaching—but you probably have the wrong impression.

Dave Busby was not your typical youth speaker. His physical appearance was not winsome. His clothes were not "cool" or trendy according to the fashion standards of the day. He was skinny in a way that can be described only as frail. As he spoke, he usually leaned on a chair or stool to support his

weakened body. And then there was the breathing. He suffered from cystic fibrosis, which forced him to take a labored
breath in a gasping kind of way—after every sentence spoken.
With each raspy inhale, the whole audience paused as his
small chest expanded dramatically, taking in enough air to
complete the next sentence. Before long, you would catch
yourself breathing in rhythm with him as if to help him along.

Dave is seemingly unique in the world of speaking the
gospel. Indeed, God did make him, gift him and use him in a
specific way to accomplish what only God could through him.
But while the details and life experiences of individual witnesses like Dave may vary greatly, the story is always the same
when it comes to speaking the good news.

Dave is no longer with us. He passed away in 1997 but his life
and ministry serve as an example for sharing our faith. It is not
our great ability to speak that causes our message to be effective.
It is not our great strength that brings power to the presentation.
It is not in our wisdom that we convince others through solid
reason and argument. No, in fact, it is the exact opposite. In
God's upside-down kingdom economy, power comes from
weakness, wisdom comes from foolishness, and effectiveness
comes from human limitations. As we share the story of Jesus
to those around us, we speak most powerfully in our weakness.

Paul's Weakness

This is what Paul is getting at in his second letter to the Corinthians when he writes about his "thorn in the flesh." He pleaded
with God to take this unknown illness or disability away, but
God refused, saying, "My grace is sufficient for you, for my
power is made perfect in weakness." Paul's response?
"Therefore, I will boast all the more gladly of my weaknesses,

so that the power of Christ may rest upon me. For the sake of Christ, then, I am content with weaknesses.... For when I am weak, then I am strong" (2 Corinthians 12:9-10). In this one statement, he summarized three major themes found in his writings to the first-century Christians living in Corinth: weakness, power and boasting. Throughout these two letters, he was attempting to redefine each of these in kingdom terms, and through his writing we gain great perspective on how we speak effectively in the name of Jesus. In short, our spiritual understanding of boasting, weakness and power dictate how we speak.

It would appear from the biblical record that the Corinthians thought pretty highly of themselves. Why were they so arrogant? It could be the prominence of their world-class commerce contributing to their vast wealth.[1] Maybe they liked to brag about their favorable geographic location; they were a city supporting two ports with an innovative transport system that pulled ships over land from the Adriatic to the Aegean Sea. They could have taken pride in any number of exported luxury items. They were known worldwide for high-quality leather, their bronze and the unique capital designs atop their columns. Or perhaps their boasting was because they were the host city to one of four major Olympic-style competitions known as the Isthmian Games, which drew athletes and spectators from all over the Greek world every two years.

They certainly had a lot to be proud of, but we can't know for sure exactly what they were bragging about. Their superior attitude was obvious to one and all and even carried over into the church. It must have been obvious to the apostle who ministered to them, because he talked about boasting a lot. The words *boast* and *boasting* are found thirty-nine times in the New Testament, and twenty-six of those times are in Paul's writings to the Corinthians.

In 1 Corinthians 1:17, Paul began his ongoing dialogue about the message and messengers of Christ, contrasting power and weakness, and noting what they should and should not boast in. This holy instruction will serve as our guide for learning how we speak powerfully in weakness.

Boasting (Gifted Speaking)

The first thing Paul addressed in his first letter was a debate about preacher allegiances. They were actually boasting about which preacher of the gospel converted them. Some preferred the apostolic authority of Paul, others the gifted and eloquent teaching of Apollos (see Acts 18:24-28) and still others Cephas (another name for the apostle Peter, though we have no biblical indication that he ever preached there). It is clear that they took pride in and gave great worth to the ability associated with persuasive speech. Oratory was actually one of the competitions in the Isthmian Games. (I wonder if they wore uniforms?) To them, effective speaking was based on tangible talent that could be measured and compared, even when it came to sharing the gospel. In other words, preachers were either good or bad based on their abilities.

Ironically, if not intentionally, Paul employed a form of influential speaking often used in speech competitions to win an argument. He made his point by asking three rhetorical questions: "Where is the one who is wise? Where is the scribe? Where is the debater of this age?" (1 Corinthians 1:20). If these Corinthian people—who held wise men, writers and orators in such high esteem—took these questions literally, they could have actually named and located someone or several someones in each of these categories within their city. Philosophers abounded in Corinth. Writers held sway over Corinth's social consciousness. Speakers and debaters thrilled crowds daily in the forums, theaters and government halls.

But Paul's line of questioning wasn't an attempt to get a list of names. Instead he was trying to make a spiritual point. He wanted these first-century believers to acknowledge that great philosophers, writers and debaters don't last. Those who boast and brag today and those we boast and brag about will likely be forgotten within years of their death. Often it's sooner than that. Influence based on human talent is fleeting, and adoring fans are fickle, but the wisdom of God remains. In fact, human wisdom is not only forgotten, but God turns it into foolishness. God says "I will destroy the wisdom of the wise," (1 Corinthians 1:19). And besides, it wasn't all that smart anyway. "For the foolishness of God is wiser than men" (1 Corinthians 1:25). As I have said before, when Albert Einstein said, "E=MC^2," God said, "Duh!"

So, what are the implications for speaking, preaching and proclaiming in the twenty-first century in light of this boasting? Only that our message is not based on our own doing or on any ability that we might take pride in. You see, even when we share the salvation story, boasting can find its way in. Some tell their story in a way that subtly sensationalizes their past to impress Christian friends. Others share their story in such a way that highlights their great faith and how hard they are working for God. Some display a boastful attitude as they lean on their charismatic personality to win people with their wit and charm. Still others take pride in their capacity for knowledge and their ability to reason and prepare an intelligent response to every spiritual question.

Even preachers can get caught up in celebrity status based on their popularity in declaring the word of God. But none of us has done anything that is worthy of bragging about.

The Spirit affirmed this through Paul when he wrote that salvation happened in such a way that "no human being might boast in the presence of God" (1 Corinthians 1:29). All the work of the story we share and even the ability to share it comes from God who has made us wise through Jesus, righteous through Jesus, holy through Jesus and saved through Jesus. What could *we* possibly brag about?

As we speak to this world with the message of Jesus Christ, it should be evident that our best strategy is to brag on God. He's the one who deserves credit. He's the one who did all the work. His power alone could make it happen. He will never fail or waiver. Go ahead, witness by bragging a little about your God. Or as Paul said it, "Let the one who boasts, boast in the Lord" (1 Corinthians 1:31; see also 2 Corinthians 10:17; Jeremiah 9:24).

Weaknesses (Limitations for Speaking)

Not only did Paul encourage Christians not to brag, but he also pointed out the weaknesses we bring to the evangelism equation. In the case of the Corinthian church, he was giving them a dose of humility—reminding them where they came from. But his encouragement to "consider your calling" in 1 Corinthians 1:26 is also useful to those of us who find our-selves on the other end of the confidence spectrum. For some, the problem isn't bragging; it's a lack of confidence that keeps them from proclaiming the gospel.

For braggers and low self-esteemers alike, these statements remind us that we all come from a position of weakness. In one sentence, Paul reminds us that none of us is qualified or worthy when it comes to our calling: "Not many of you were wise according to worldly standards, not many were powerful, not many were of noble birth" (1 Corinthians 1:26). These three "qualifications"—worldly wisdom, power and pedigree—can be a stumbling block to both the overconfident and the timid when it comes to sharing the gospel.

Paul pointed out that none of the Corinthians were wise when they came to faith in Christ. This may give us some insight into the makeup of the church: that there were no philosophers or orators among them. It may be that they were a group of pretty common people. Frankly, most churches are made up of average people. This is a good reminder for those who feel like they aren't smart enough to have a voice in the spiritual dialogue of our time. In fact, when speaking about God or for God, no one is wise, so we all find ourselves in the same spiritual boat. Even Paul, though he was an educated man, reminded these followers that he did not preach the gospel "with words of eloquent wisdom " (1 Corinthians 1:17). Sharing our faith is not about wisdom.

But wisdom was not the only thing lacking in the Corinthians' pedigree. He reminded them that not many were powerful. Again, we are not exactly sure what Paul meant by this, for surely there were people of influence in the church. We do know that there was a guy named Erastus who was a Christian and also a Corinthian public official (see Romans 16:23). But in terms of social and military power or political influence, the church in Corinth doesn't appear to have been made up of people who were movers and shakers.

There are Christians today who readily identify with this seeming lack of social and physical power. They often bemoan the fact that they do not have the necessary authority or influence to change the culture in which they live. Or they wish they could exhibit some sort of Holy Spirit power in their lives that would influence others. Our culture (like that of the Jews in 1 Corinthians 1:22) often demands signs, and many Christ-followers just don't believe they have the power to bring a spiritual "wow factor" as they share the gospel. Often we find ourselves believing in the power of the resurrection, but not that such power could be evident in our lives.

And yet one more "weakness" remains. Paul said that not many were of "noble birth." In other words, not many members of First Christian Church in Corinth could claim to be part of the social elite. Not many of them had royal blood. Nor did they carry official titles. They didn't live in palatial homes, nor were they members of the wealthiest merchant and landowning families. As in many churches of the first century, many were likely slaves, women and Jews who all found themselves on the lower rungs of the social ladder.

In our times, many people feel unworthy as evangelists because they aren't executives, managers, coaches or bosses. They are sure that no one will listen to what they have to say about Jesus because no one really listens to them anyway. Convincing people that they are leaders is a great challenge. It's true that not everyone inspires or gives direction to the masses. Not everyone has a title or a name that carries authority. Most aren't in a position to set directions for businesses or organizations, but everyone influences someone. In that sense, everyone leads.

Most Christians don't have wisdom, power, or pedigree, and that's a good thing. When it comes to speaking for God, we should learn to embrace the reasons we can't, because weakness is what God uses best. Moses stuttered but became

God's spokesperson. Gideon was weak but became God's mighty warrior. David was just a shepherd but became God's king. Not very wise? "God chose what is foolish in the world to shame the wise." Not strong enough? "God chose what is weak in the world to shame the strong" (1 Corinthians 1:27). Are you just a nobody? "God chose what is low and despised in the world, even things that are not, to bring to nothing the things that are" (v. 28).

Power (Life-Changing Speaking)

Like our Corinthian brothers and sisters, we need to change our understanding of power. They saw power in the visible things they could boast in, like worldly wisdom, influence and smooth talk. We see power in visible things that others applaud: success, wealth, celebrity and political power. But for the Christian, none of these things holds power. As we have already mentioned above, God sees all of our power as weak. But in a paradox that can be described only as God-sized, he not only laughs at our power, but also demonstrates his power through something we consider weak. This weakness is "a stumbling block to Jews and folly to Gentiles" (1 Corinthians 1:23), but it is the power behind every conversation you and I ever dare to have concerning our faith. The power is in the cross.

We confidently assert with the apostle this power of the cross:

- If we rely on our eloquence and wisdom to speak, we empty the cross of Christ of its power. There is simply nothing more powerful we can say than to speak of the cross. (See 1 Corinthians 1:17.)

- The only powerful word we need to know to evangelize the world is the story of the cross. "For the word of the cross is folly to those who are perishing, but to us who are being saved it is the power of God" (1 Corinthians 1:18).

- The message we proclaim is Jesus Christ, crucified to take away our sin and give us eternal life through his resurrection. "But we preach Christ crucified . . . to those who are called, both Jews and Greeks, Christ the power of God and the wisdom of God" (1 Corinthians 1:23-24).

We don't have to be smarter than the world to be a witness. We don't have to have political, military or social power to make an eternal difference in our world. We don't have to be articulate, passionate, relevant or intelligent. We simply acknowledge our weaknesses because they become our collective testimony. All we have to do is point others to the place where we have found salvation—namely, the cross of Jesus. For when we testify to this, we speak powerfully in weakness.

Week Four

Devotional Readings

....

MONDAY
We Speak Powerfully in Weakness

> *For the foolishness of God is wiser than men, and the*
> *weakness of God is stronger than men.*
>
> 1 CORINTHIANS 1:25

Weakness is not one of those words most people quickly embrace. We prefer terms like *strength, vigor, might* and *power*. A large part of Western Christianity has been flooded with a health, wealth and prosperity doctrine that fundamentally lacks the cross of Jesus Christ. Apparently the Corinthian Christians were susceptible to the same kind of false teaching. They were enamored with all the wrong things: eloquence, intellectual abilities, supernatural gifts, polished personalities and ecstatic experiences. Paul would have none of this nonsense. He boldly and uncompromisingly declared that real eloquence, real intelligence and real power reside not in the things of this world, but in the crucified Christ. The message of the cross can seem so irrelevant to a world marked by pride and human reason. It just looks and sounds profoundly weak.

I don't know if you have ever been laughed at because of your faith in Jesus Christ. Years ago, while attending a discipleship conference in Ocean City, Maryland, I engaged a Boston intellectual (that's how he described himself) in a spiritual conversation along the ocean's boardwalk. I spoke of a God so wise that he was willing to appear so silly by hanging on a cross for us. The Bostonian laughed aloud. Our weaknesses are obvious: we are not wise by human standards, not powerful by human measurements and not special from the world's point of view. We are weak, but he is strong.

Week Four

TUESDAY
Not Eloquent

> *For Christ did not send me to baptize but to preach the*
> *gospel, and not with words of eloquent wisdom,*
> *lest the cross of Christ be emptied of its power.*
>
> 1 CORINTHIANS 1:17

Paul's words are utterly simple and undeniably profound. This wise apostle was saying, "I don't care about polished style." Please notice with me that Paul was not shrinking the importance of Christian baptism. What he was doing was elevating the cross of Jesus Christ. He was attempting to shock the Corinthians, and perhaps us, into seeing the folly of eloquent speech that is divorced from Jesus dying on the cross.

Apparently Paul's critics argued that he could be deep and dull. He gave their criticism little weight. What he most cared about was making the gospel crystal clear. Christ, according to Paul, was, is and forever shall be God's Logos. *Logos* is the Greek word for "rhetoric," "speech," "reason" or "word." Paul took that term and attached it to Jesus Christ, who is the one supreme Word that matters. One verse later, he reminded his readers that there are only two kinds of people: those who are choosing to perish and those who are choosing to be saved. Paul was declaring, with incredible irony, that God uses his

Word—not slick and polished words—to save. When we trust eloquence rather than Christ, we empty the cross of its power.

As I mentioned earlier, I was a stutterer. My childhood was marked by the inability to complete a sentence. I never imagined that God would one day fashion me into a teacher and preacher. Perhaps you sense your own limitations today. You and I are not called to be eloquent, but to trust entirely the finished work of Jesus. We speak of Him.

Week Four

WEDNESDAY
Not Wise

For since, in the wisdom of God, the world did not know
God through wisdom, it pleased God through the
folly of what we preach to save those who believe.

1 CORINTHIANS 1:21

Yesterday's devotional was a reminder that Paul did not care about polished style. Today's verse makes it clear that the apostle's I-don't-care list also included professional scholarship. But please don't jump to conclusions prematurely. Paul was not an anti-intellectual. After all, we know he studied under the famous Jewish rabbinic intellectual Gamaliel (Acts 22:3). Paul was not resistant to advanced education. What he rejected, without hesitation, was human reason—man at the center of his own universe.

The apostle quoted Isaiah 29:14 just in front of today's passage. That Old Testament text was intended to illustrate the ridiculousness of human arrogance. Sennacherib, the king of Assyria, and his vast army had surrounded King Hezekiah and the city of Jerusalem. Things looked hopeless. After all, Sennacherib had defeated every other army he had faced. Isaiah 29 and the parallel passages in 2 Kings 18–19 and 2 Chronicles 32 elevate the pompous pride of this Darth Vader–

like ruler. But God soundly defeated Sennacherib. The cross, according to Paul, is a contradiction to human wisdom and arrogance.

Do you recall the smartest kid in your school? My high school, located in a small southern Illinois town, was preoccupied with the National Honor Society—a good and noble organization that recognizes the best and brightest students based on scholarship, leadership, service and character. The problem in my town was that some students cheated to get selected to the NHS. True wisdom is found in Christ, not human academic achievement. As Mike wrote earlier, "we don't have to be smarter than the world" to speak for Christ.

Week Four

THURSDAY
Not Supernatural or Sensible

For Jews demand signs and Greeks seek wisdom.

1 CORINTHIANS 1:22

We are defined by the God we worship. The apostle Paul had a no-nonsense view of the world. On one hand, he saw his own people, the Jews, wanting something from God in order to believe that Jesus was the Messiah. "Show us a sign"—that's what the religious leaders of Jesus' day asked of him (Matthew 12:38; Mark 8:11; Luke 11:16; John 6:30). Paul had little tolerance for anyone needing a miracle in order to believe. On the other hand, the Greek world was zealous for all kinds of learning. They were, after all, a civilization of great philosophers and educators, drunk on the telling or hearing of the newest ideas (Acts 17:21). Reason was their god. These two basic and fundamental idols, the supernatural and the sensible, permeated Paul's world. They are still alive and well and passionately worshiped in the twenty-first century.

The cross of Jesus stands in opposition to both of these idols. Jesus-followers see the world differently. We don't need a supernatural sign or a sensible reason. We believe in a one-of-a-kind story. When I was a boy, I loved fairy tales and Viking myths. Because readers of books were not celebrated in my community, I would sneak off to the library after football practice; I didn't want to have to defend my reasons for reading. Those stories of riches, dragons, heroes and villains captured my heart. Then, through the lips of an ordinary person, I heard for the first time that the God of the universe loved me so much that he sent his only Son to die for me. I believed. How about you?

We speak a story.

Week Four

FRIDAY
Not Status

God chose what is low and despised in the world, even things
that are not, to bring to nothing things that are, so that no
human being might boast in the presence of God.

All of us are prone to boasting. Years ago as a young pastor, I got suckered into a brag-fest among some of the high school students. The little church I served had a basement where Sunday school was held. Two separate sets of staircases, one in the front of the basement and one in the back of the basement, made for a perfect racetrack. The idea was to see how fast you could run from the top of the back staircase, down into the basement, up the front staircase, through the worship auditorium and to the starting step. What was kept secret, until I had succumbed to boasting that *I* could run faster than anyone else, was that the race was conducted in complete darkness. To make a rather long story short, I crashed and burned at the bottom of the first staircase. I ran into the wall, broke my glasses, bloodied my face and swallowed my pride.

God, it turns out, is not interested in our boasting. He quite intentionally chose all the things that we would reject in order to accomplish his great purpose and plan. God specifically

selected a Roman cross—a stumbling block to Jews and foolishness to Gentiles—as his primary means of putting the fractured world of sin and death back together. Our goodness,
church attendance, Sunday offerings, acts of benevolence,
intelligence, popularity or power could not and cannot save
us. God forever removed from us any possibility of standing
before him and boasting that we saved ourselves. We speak
of what only God can do.

five

We Speak of
Hope in Suffering

D r. Robert Black was a well-respected professor of Old Testament for several decades at Johnson University in Knoxville, Tennessee. His gruff lecture style, impromptu pop quizzes, lengthy study guides (called "key questions") and daily roll call could initially be intimidating, but the twinkle in his eye and quick wit belied his playful soul and made him a student favorite. Just when you thought he was simply reading his notes, he would throw in a quotable phrase or humorous social reference that revealed his gift for communicating.

One such phrase (repeated many times to hundreds of students throughout the years) was actually a clever one-line testimony of who he was. "I was born in Hope and I will die in hope," he often stated with conviction. This singular sentence told his entire life story. It referenced that he was born in Hope, Indiana, and it was also a testament to his life of following Christ and the hope found in him. Hope was an integral part of Dr. Black's story from birth to grave. This is not an indication that his life was free of suffering—it certainly wasn't—but his whole life was lived in hope, and for him that made all the difference.

And this is the point of the message we proclaim. Hope doesn't take the suffering away; it simply allows us to find joy in the same circumstances in which others find despair. So we speak of hope in a world filled with suffering.

Hope in Suffering

The apostle Peter wrote the first letter bearing his name to a group of Christians he called "exiles of the Dispersion" (1 Peter 1:1) who had been "scattered" (1:1 NIV) throughout the northern parts of Asia Minor (modern-day Turkey). And throughout this letter he speaks of suffering. Ten times in five chapters he uses a form of the Greek word *paschō*, which has to do with feeling—especially the bad kind. The indication from these verses is that most of their suffering was a direct result of persecution for their faith, their status as foreigners or a combination of both. The apostle wrote, "But even if you should suffer for righteousness' sake, you will be blessed. . . . For it is better to suffer for doing good if that should be God's will, than for doing evil" (1 Peter 3:14, 17).

It seems the message is that suffering is inevitable, but "Peter's pastoral purpose is to help these early believers see their temporary sufferings in the full light of the coming eternal glory."[1] In other words, he tells them that they have something those in the world (who also suffer) do not have. And that something is hope. According to Scriptures, Christ-followers have hope that the suffering will end. And these two together, suffering and hope, become a vehicle for our witness. "In your hearts honor Christ the Lord as holy, always being prepared to make a defense to anyone who asks you for a reason for the hope that is in you" (1 Peter 3:15). In other words, the answers we give for our hope are often most powerfully expressed in our suffering.

This world is filled with suffering, you know? Suffering is part of the fallen human condition, and since this world is inhabited by over seven billion human beings, suffering abounds. Everyone reading this page right now has suffered, will suffer or is suffering right now. There are different levels of suffering and it comes in many different forms, to be sure, but absolutely no one (including Jesus-followers) is exempt.

Suffering from Poverty

Some suffer as a result of extreme poverty. We live in a global community that includes countries like the Congo, Zimbabwe and Burundi. These three are the poorest of the world's countries (based on Gross Domestic Product in 2013), with each person's average yearly worth estimated to be under $700.[2] In economies like these, citizens can't count on even their most basic needs being met. In these countries and dozens like them, families live in makeshift homes constructed of cardboard boxes, aluminum sheets and scrap wood. Children daily scrounge through trash heaps and polluted streams, looking for something to fill their empty bellies. Every day millions go to bed hungry and many starve to death. To add to this daily despair, there are no prospects for employment, income or a change in their situation.

Godly people are not immune to this suffering. Many of us have traveled to poor countries on short-term mission trips and had our hearts broken as we have witnessed firsthand the poverty of those we minister to and with. Children of godly men and women go without clothes and shoes. Church families cram into one-room shanties. Praying parents can't afford medical care for their sick children. These are brothers and sisters in Christ suffering from extreme poverty who long for the scraps that you and I throw away.

Even in the Bible, the famous story of the widow's mite reminds us that godly people experience poverty just like nonbelievers (see Luke 21:1-3). Jesus noted that this woman was faithful in her worship, sacrificial in her giving and humble in her demeanor, but her economic value was represented by two worthless coins revealing that she lived in daily poverty.

Suffering from Poor Health

Much of the world's suffering has to do with health-related issues. To be sure, much of the world's diseases are a direct result of poverty, but everyone—rich and poor—is vulnerable to illness. Probably every one of us has a friend or family member who has been diagnosed with some form of cancer. This singular disease remains one of the biggest fears for those of us who don't have it. And it brings incredible suffering on those who do experience the pain of the advancing disease or the treatments used to heal it. And this is only cancer.

People suffer from accidents that break bones and tear ligaments, necessitating months of rehab. Many suffer due to internal organ failure and subsequent surgeries ranging from heart bypasses to appendectomies, and they suffer the recuperation that comes with each. Still others experience daily back pain, headaches, arthritis, sprained ankles, pulled hamstrings and toothaches. Simply put, life in this world hurts for everyone, including those who follow Jesus.

One of Paul's dear friends, Epaphroditus, experienced serious illness. When Paul wrote his letter to the Christians at

Philippi, he gave them a health update on their friend and church representative. Apparently news of his life-threatening illness had gotten back to the folks at home. Paul wrote, "Indeed he was ill, near to death" (Philippians 2:27). I've always wondered why this apostle who had healed hundreds didn't just heal his friend. For whatever reason he didn't, and this reminds us that sometimes Christians like Epaphroditus in the first century and those of us in this century deal with pain from physical illness.

Suffering Mentally and Emotionally

Still others experience mental and emotional suffering. Many go through every day finding it hard to love and be loved as a result of abuse suffered as a child or from former unhealthy relationships. Millions of people hold internal fears, either real or imagined, that keep them from functioning in normal activities like going to school, work or public gatherings. A growing number of people sink into severe depression as a result of these fears, and often many years of counseling and therapy are required to help them survive.

Though it has often been held that Christians don't suffer from this type of suffering, believers do in fact deal with the spiritual challenges that come with anxiety, fear and depression. Fortunately, churches have graduated from being judgmental to providing and recommending Christian counseling and therapy for Christ-followers.

Sarah the wife of Abraham suffered emotionally as a result of her barren condition and the mess she and her husband made by bringing her handmaid into the relationship. In a speech revealing her inner turmoil resulting from her handmaid's son, she passionately said, "May the wrong done to me be on you!" (Genesis 16:5). Like many, she struggled with deep emotional pain that had been suppressed for years, and she represents many who truly believe in God but still experience emotional instability.

Suffering from Persecution

Finally, humans experience suffering at the hands of other human beings. Physical bullying often begins in the playgrounds and streets of childhood and early adolescence as bullies force their wills on everyone else. As newscasts and headlines often reveal, the crimes escalate from schoolyard fights to gang drivebys, genocide and war. From the time of Cain and Abel, the third and fourth human beings in history, humans have inflicted pain and suffering on others. And as in this first uprising, it is often the unrighteous against the righteous.

Christianity was birthed in suffering. Persecution from the Jewish leaders and then the Roman Empire, and a two-millennia succession of enemies has included prejudice, social separation, jailing, beating and often death. In Acts 7 we find the first martyr in the biblical record persecuted to the point of death because of his faith in Jesus. Stephen was brutally put to death by stoning after a sermon in which he testified concerning Jesus. As we noted earlier, *martyr* (from *martyreō*) originally meant simply "to testify" but came to define someone who dies for his or her testimony. Stephen would not be the last martyr. As the church learned, to proclaim Christ in the first century was a dangerous proposition.

In light of this Bible story, I've always joked that preachers are just one bad sermon away from their congregation stoning them. But this is no joke. The story continues: "There arose on that day a great persecution against the church in Jerusalem, and they were all scattered" (Acts 8:1). It may have been these scattered ones who Peter is addressing in his letter; we can't be sure. What we do know is that from that fateful day in Jerusalem to the present, Christians have suffered physical harm and persecution from passionate opponents of the church. In a 2014 report by Open Doors, a nondenominational organization supporting persecuted Christians, said it documented 2,123 "martyr" killings worldwide in 2013, with 1,213 of those deaths in Syria. The report went on to say that Christianity "faces restrictions and hostility in 111 countries."[3]

While Western Christians may not face such deadly forms of persecution, they are often marginalized in their culture, silenced in their workplace, ostracized from social circles and judged for holding to their beliefs. Is this truly suffering as expressed in this passage from Peter? Probably not, but there is no doubt that Christians suffer. Some more, some less. Some physically and mentally, others from poverty and persecution.

Along with other Bible passages, 1 Peter 3:15 reminds us that whatever the suffering, Christians have a different outlook from others who suffer. This outlook, this hope, becomes an opportunity for us to speak of our faith in Jesus. Hope is the antidote to suffering. I don't think it's overstating it to say that hope is the great separation between unbelievers who suffer and Christians who suffer.

Let's return to 1 Peter 3:15 and look at the word *hope*. It is a Greek word (*elpis*) that means to anticipate and expect good to come. Paul reminded the Ephesians that without Jesus they had no hope: "Remember that you were at one time separated from Christ, alienated from the commonwealth of Israel and strangers to the covenants of promise, having no hope and without God in the world" (Ephesians 2:12). On the other hand, "we know that for those who love God all things work together for good" (Romans 8:28). This expectation comes in the context of the hope we patiently wait for (see Romans 8:24-28).

In a world of suffering, this kind of hope is curious and often spurs conversations about why we hold on to hope. Our coworkers know that we have been diagnosed with cancer. Classmates observe our reaction to being cut from the team or not making the band. Neighbors watch from a distance when we lose our job. Doctors and nurses notice how we conduct ourselves when our child is critically ill. The world wants to know why we deal with these and many other situations so differently. Are you suffering? Are you ready to speak? Soon someone will ask, and you will speak of hope even in the midst of your suffering.

Why would a widow give her last two coins as an act of worship? For the same reason someone who is laid off continues to give an offering every Sunday in worship. Because we have our eyes enlightened by the Spirit that we "may know what is the hope to which he has called [us], what are the riches of his glorious inheritance in the saints" (Ephesians 1:18). The message of Christian hope to a poverty-stricken world is that there is an eternal inheritance that can't be taken away, never fades and awaits those of us who are in Christ Jesus.

Why would a guy like Epaphroditus have hope even as he lay feverishly dying far away from home? Why would Christians who are under hospice care as cancer completes its work in their physical body still want Scripture to be read or a hymn to be sung? Because "after you have suffered a little while, the God of all grace, who has called you to his eternal glory in Christ, will himself restore, confirm, strengthen, and establish you" (1 Peter 5:10). The way Christians hope in the midst of illness, injury and pain is often a powerful testimony to those around them. Simply clinging to our faith in times like these can speak volumes.

Why would a godly woman like Abraham's wife, Sarah, continue through the daily emotional pain of childlessness? Why would Christians continue to pray and live literally one day at a time as they experience serious fears and internal doubts? Thankfully, we get insight to Sarah's faith in Hebrews 11:11: "By faith Sarah herself received power to conceive, even when she was past the age, since she considered him faithful who had promised." Our continued trust in God that he will be faithful keeps us going even if we don't feel like it. "Therefore let those who suffer according to God's will entrust their souls to a faithful Creator while doing good" (1 Peter 4:19).

And finally, why would Stephen, as he was being killed, pray for those who were stoning him, "Lord, do not hold this sin against them" (Acts 7:60)? Why would Christian evangelists start churches in villages and towns all over the world under threat of death or imprisonment? Because, as Paul says, "since we have such a hope, we are very bold" (2 Corinthians 3:12). Christians are able to speak with confidence in suffering because of the hope of eternal life. In godly anticipation that our earthly life will be followed with an eternal life, we can face persecution in a different way. If dying means life, we can boldly speak in the middle of suffering.

The greatest example of hope in the midst of suffering comes from our Lord Jesus Christ. His rejection and betrayal, his emotional turmoil while praying in the garden and his crucifixion call us to witness in the same way. "For to this you have been called, because Christ also suffered for you, leaving

you an example, so that you might follow in his steps" (1 Peter
2:21). Suffering aligns us with Christ in our human experience,
and it is his suffering on our behalf that brings us hope of
eternal life. "For the grace of God has appeared bringing salvation for all people, training us to renounce ungodliness and
worldly passions, and to live self-controlled, upright, and
godly lives in the present age, waiting for our blessed hope,
the appearing of the glory of our great God and Savior Jesus
Christ" (Titus 2:11-13). And so we live, often in suffering, and
we speak of the hope we have.

Week Five

Devotional Readings

....

MONDAY
A Prepared Hope

> *But in your hearts honor Christ the Lord as holy,*
> *always being prepared to make a defense to anyone*
> *who asks you for a reason for the hope that is in you;*
> *yet do it with gentleness and respect.*

1 PETER 3:15

As Mike mentioned earlier in this chapter, "Hope doesn't take the suffering away; it simply allows us to find joy in the same circumstances in which others find despair." Preparation is the key. Peter makes that abundantly clear in today's verse. *Prepared* (*hetoimos* in Greek), often translated as "ready," is the word I want you to notice. It is used in two distinct ways in the New Testament: of *things* like a wedding feast (Matthew 22:4, 8), an upper room (Mark 14:15), a banquet (Luke 14:17) or a cross-cultural offering (2 Corinthians 9:5); and of *people* who are ready for Christ's return (Matthew 24:44; Luke 12:40) or ready for "every good work" (Titus 3:1). For us, then, what does a prepared hope look like?

I have a morning routine. Perhaps you do too. I pray at my bedside before I do anything else. I stumble my way to the bathroom; shave; brush my teeth; put on my workout clothes; lift some weights; walk; return home; cool down; shower; dress; enter into a time of Bible reading, prayer and worship; enjoy some coffee and a light breakfast; pray some more; maybe have a little more coffee with my wife; kiss her good-bye and head to my office. My heart is ready most days to encounter whoever and whatever God has in mind. My heart is prepared to speak whether I encounter suffering or not because I have spent time with the One who speaks to me.

Week Five

TUESDAY
A Living Hope

Blessed be the God and Father of our Lord Jesus Christ!
According to his great mercy, he has caused us
to be born again to a living hope through the
resurrection of Jesus Christ from the dead.

1 PETER 1:3

Let's be perfectly clear on this Tuesday. Because of Jesus' resurrection and our new birth in and through him, we have a living hope. Again, I remind you of what Mike has written: "Hope is the antidote to suffering." Regardless of what this day may bring, whether it be cancer, divorce, the loss of a job, the death of a loved one or even persecution because of our faith in Jesus, our hope is secure and well. Our spiritual wealth in Christ remains indestructible because of his finished work at the cross. Praise his name! We bless God. We speak well of him. We "eulogize" him because of what he has done for us in Christ.

My wife and I bought a house several years ago that needed a lot of landscaping. We formulated a plan and began to work our plan. We planted perennials of various kinds, relocated bushes and prairie grass, planted a tree, restored a backyard deck, had a patio and fence built, and did all the right things a steward of God's creation should do. But some of our plants died. A harsh winter and some pesky bugs took their toll.

The Jesus-following life can be just as treacherous. We can do all the right things. We can place our trust in the One who knows us and loves us, yet sin, death and persecution can seek to devour all hope. Our hope, though, is the living kind, and we speak of that which cannot be destroyed.

Week Five

WEDNESDAY
A Battle-Ready Hope

*Preparing your minds for action, and being sober-minded,
set your hope fully on the grace that will be brought
to you at the revelation of Jesus Christ.*

1 PETER 1:13

A spiritual battle of colossal proportions has been fought since Genesis 3. Peter openly acknowledged this fact with reminders of an adversary that "prowls around like a roaring lion, seeking someone to devour" (1 Peter 5:8). Most of us have seen those *National Geographic* specials that graphically depict the ability of lions to identify, remove and consume an antelope or wildebeest from a herd. In the same way, our enemy, the devil, often uses suffering as an isolating experience. Today's passage is a sobering reminder of this war's reality. The vivid language of 1 Peter 1:13 is a valid exhortation to stay awake, be alert and always be armed for battle. Our call is to think Christianly. We are to disengage our mind from anything that would make us susceptible to the enemy's attacks and to engage our mind in everything that would keep us attached to Jesus.

Years ago, while in the military, I learned a lasting spiritual lesson: constant readiness requires regular training. As mil-

itary policemen, we were tested routinely. We endured simu-
lated attacks in order to be ready if and when the real thing
surfaced. We rehearsed and repeated the same tactics until
they became a part of our muscle memory. One night the real
thing did happen. A terrorist unsuccessfully attempted to infil-
trate the fence line of the NATO base we were protecting. Our
readiness stood the test. In the same way, real Jesus-followers
inherit and maintain a battle-ready hope. We speak of a hope
grounded in Christ's return, even as the battle continues.

Week Five

THURSDAY
A Grounded Hope

> *He was foreknown before the foundation of the world,*
> *but was made manifest in the last times for the sake of you*
> *who through him are believers in God, who raised him*
> *from the dead and gave him glory, so that*
> *your faith and hope are in God.*

1 PETER 1:20-21

I love thinking about the greatness and grandeur of God. Before he spoke the world into existence, God planned it all out. He knew exactly when he would send his one and only Son, born of a virgin, who suffered under Pontius Pilate, was tempted just like us, yet without sin, was able to sympathize with us, able to defeat sin and death on the cross and more than able to transform us into his likeness. He was crucified, buried, raised and ascended. Our hope as Jesus-followers is grounded hope. It is historic (important) and historical (real). We have the inexpressible joy of living on this side of the cross. Jesus' resurrection is the basis on which we so joyfully anticipate our future reward.

Most all of us hope. We hope for safety, good health, peace, happiness and prosperity. More than anything, we hope for love. You might recall Andy Dufresne (played by Tim Robbins), the innocent convict in the highly acclaimed film *Shawshank Redemption.* Despair surrounds every part of this prison story. A corrupt warden and sadistic guards make life in Shawshank intolerable. But Andy dares to speak of hope. His friend Red (Morgan Freeman) warns of the dangers of hope. In the end, though, Andy writes these memorable words to Red, "Remember, Red, hope is a good thing, maybe the best of things, and no good thing ever dies." Like Andy, we cling to hope. However, our hope is grounded in Christ. We dare to speak of it and him.

Week Five

FRIDAY
A Fulfilled Hope

And after you have suffered a little while, the God of all grace,
who has called you to his eternal glory in Christ, will himself
restore, confirm, strengthen, and establish you.

1 PETER 5:10

Suffering and grace are an odd pair. They resemble a frog and a princess. They are divine oil and water seemingly unable to mix. But in God's strange economy, suffering and grace not only go together, they are inseparable. Peter acknowledged this by openly speaking of suffering's reality, especially for those who live under the lordship of Jesus Christ. I've gone through my English Bible and marked the nineteen occasions in which Peter inserted a reminder about the "various trials" (1:6), "sorrows" (2:19), "fiery trial" (4:12) and suffering (1:11; 2:19, 20, 21, 23; 3:14, 17, 18; 4:1 twice; 4:13, 15, 16, 19; 5:9, 10) that Jesus and his followers have faced, are facing and will face. Just as intentionally, Peter strategically inserted *grace* eight times, as a reminder of what sustains us in seasons of suffering (1:2, 10, 13; 4:10; 5:5, 10, 12). Suffering and grace are a reminder that one day our hope will be fulfilled.

No one travels far in life without colliding with suffering. I was eight years old when my mother lost a baby boy. My brother died shortly after his first breath. I recall the heartache that blanketed our home. My mother's faith in a God who is not precarious or mean allowed her to embrace grace, and she carried on by facing her grief and surrendering to her Lord. One day she will be reunited with my brother and so will I. We speak of hope fulfilled, because we place our faith in a God who keeps his promises.

six

We Speak
Throughout Our Lives

In August of 2011, a preaching video of Kanon Tipton became an overnight YouTube sensation. The footage of his sermon was recorded as he spoke in front of a Mississippi congregation, and it led to several television appearances. What made him special? He is a third-generation preacher, and he was four years old—the "world's youngest preacher." On the other end of the spectrum is Samuel Akinbode Sadela, who at 111 years was still preaching weekly at Christ Gospel Apostolic Church in Lagos, Nigeria. Amazingly, he has been preaching at this same church for almost eighty years. These two preachers, who represent opposite ends of the "we speak" spectrum illustrate that in the church both young and old can speak.

As I understand the biblical picture of the family of God, every generation is designed to function in and speak into the life of the church. Yet it can often be hard for a generation to find its voice, and this is mostly felt by the generations on either end of the age spectrum—namely, the young and the old. This difficulty may be because each of these age categories carries with it significant stereotypes, realities and attitudes associated with each. Still, each generation has a unique opportunity to speak. We'll allow two well-known Bible characters to represent the biblical voice of each of these generations. Timothy will represent the younger generation and King David will represent the older.

Timothy: The Young Generation

A passage from the first letter that Paul wrote to Timothy, his "son in the faith," has been thoroughly taught, especially in youth ministry circles. I suppose that's because it addresses a natural gap between younger and older generations. Paul tells Timothy, "Let no one despise you for your youth" (1 Timothy 4:12). He uses the same Greek word for "despise" with another young apprentice, Titus, which the translators usually render, "Let no one disregard you" (Titus 2:15). The root word of both *despise* and *disregard* (*phroneō*) literally means to "think or comprehend down"—in other words, looking down on another or thinking of oneself as a higher-up. This tendency seems to be a natural and universal response from older, more experienced people to those of a younger generation. Obviously, these young leaders were looked down on in the first-century church, and not much has changed in two thousand years.

Then, as now, older people often despise or disregard young people simply because they are young and inexperienced. This is true in everyday life, and it can be true within relationships in the body of Christ. Sometimes this disregarding can be subtle. Older generations may choose not to support the efforts of a young person who has new and passionate ideas, thereby stifling his or her influence in the church by failing to listen to younger voices and by not inviting them into conversations that matter. Sometimes the despising comes as a double-edged compliment: "Someday you're going to be a great leader" (which really means, "Today is not that day").

This bias against a younger generation is sometimes much more straightforward. How many times has someone from a more experienced generation remarked to a young leader, "You don't have the experience" or "You have a lot to learn" or the dreaded "When I was your age . . . "? In fact, the church, through policy and culture, often prevents the inclusion of younger voices on boards, committees and ministry teams. This prohibits an entire generation from being heard. The assumption is that those with little experience are not capable of valuable input, which effectively silences an entire generation.

We don't know for sure what was happening in the first-century church at Ephesus where Timothy appears to be the young pastor/leader. Maybe Paul knew of a specific situation where he was called into question due to his youth. Or maybe Paul remembered some crusty old colleagues who were likely to give Timothy a hard time. It could even be that Paul was encouraging Timothy regarding his timidity as some other passages may hint at (see 2 Timothy 1:7). It could be all of the above, but more than likely he was simply experiencing the gap that has always existed between older and younger generations.

For this reason, these short verses of instruction to the young man Timothy (1 Timothy 4:12 in particular) have become an inspirational and useful guideline for a younger generation in the church. These inspired words are incredibly helpful for those who, like Timothy, find themselves trying to discover their voice among those within the fellowship who have more experience and as a result more wisdom. While Timothy may not be typical of most young Christians, since he seems to hold the role of preacher/leader in the first-century church at Ephesus, the advice that the apostle gives his young apprentice is practical advice for *all* Christian young people. We will examine this passage in an effort to find concrete instruction for how young people can legitimately have a voice in the church and thereby say, "We speak."

But before we get to the teaching, you may be wondering just how old Timothy was when he was put into this leadership role and Paul wrote him these letters. The Bible is inconclusive on his age, but it does give some clues. We know that he was a Christian living in Lystra when Paul recruited him in Acts 16 for missions work, and we can place the date of this letter about eleven years after this occasion. So if he was a twenty-year-old when he began with Paul, we could reasonably guess him to be about thirty-one or even younger when Paul wrote this encouragement to him. At any rate, Paul's use of the term "my child" at the beginning of the letter would indicate someone under forty years of age (1 Timothy 1:2).

Here's the advice the apostle Paul wrote to this young leader two thousand years ago concerning how he should express himself: "Let no one despise you for your youth, but set the believers an example in speech, in conduct, in love, in faith, in purity" (4:12).

This instruction will be even more helpful with a proper understanding of the word *example*, because in its meaning we find a word picture for just how a younger generation can speak. The Greek word translated "example" here is *typos*. It literally means "to strike," but it can also indicate an image that is struck or a mark left by a strike. Think of an ancient hammer and chisel striking out a word on stone. Then think of the current English word *type*, which is literally the mark of black letters on a white page. Paul is telling Timothy that the best way for young people to influence others is to mark them, or as we might say, "leave an impression" on them. He gives five different ways a younger generation can leave their mark on the church.

1. *In speech.* Young people are to be influential in their speech. This is not to say in the actual content of their speech, but in the way they speak. Many times a young person's words are ignored because he or she uses language that leaves a bad impression. This kind of speech can include an irreverent, unappreciative tone, an arrogant attitude or even crude or questionable slang. The best way to find an audience with an older generation is to pay attention to these common message killers.

If you want to speak in the church, begin with a humble attitude that celebrates the work and faith of the saints who have gone before you. Young people display wisdom when they appreciate that they don't have the only good ideas and that they are standing on a faith foundation that others have built. As for the crude speech that is prevalent in our culture—right or wrong—when those from an older generation hear certain words from a younger person, they immediately disqualify him or her as someone to be heard. Work to clean these words out of your vocabulary for the sake of holiness and to increase your voice.

2. *In conduct.* Those who are in their teens, twenties and thirties can be heard loudest by the life that they live. We have all heard the adage "Actions speak louder than words," and never is this truer than when it comes to living a life of faith. As a young person, what do your actions say to those in the congregation in which you serve? Are you involved in the church's workdays, showing that you are willing to put your faith into action? Do you show up for all-church prayer

meetings? Is it evident that you are a Christian in the workplace? Do people see you bringing your friends to church and
leading them to faith and baptism? All of these ways in which
you conduct your life and many more can speak volumes to
those of a different generation. What does your life say?

3. In love. Loving others is another great way for a young
person to preach without talking. The vision statement for the
church I serve in has stated it this way: "We want others to
find Jesus irresistible because of our ridiculous love." The idea
is that if we simply love others the way Christ has loved us, we
will earn the right to be heard by them. Older people may be
hesitant to follow the lead of a younger voice, but they are
likely to listen to anyone who will take the time to truly love
them. Young Christian, since love is the lead story of Jesus, it
is always good advice to love those you want to influence.
Spend time talking about their lives, dreams, fears and failures.
Pray with them. Really listen. Help in tangible ways if you can.
Give them a Christian hug and smile every time you see them.
Call them by name. Say, "I love you with the love of my Lord."
In this way, you'll find an audience who will willingly listen to
you because they know your words come from love.

4. In faith. Living a life of strong belief is yet another way to
make a great impression. Again, the tendency in our youth is to
talk about our faith, debate our faith and tell others how much
we believe. The word for faith in 1 Timothy 4:12 (*pistis* in the
Greek) means to be convicted or convinced. What you truly
believe about Jesus as Lord and Savior is revealed in the normal
circumstances of life. In other words, young Christian, how
does your faith hold up when you experience the setback of an
illness or loss? What does your trust in Jesus look like when you
are looking for the right Christian spouse or when you are a new

parent raising small children? What does your faith look like when Christians and others observe you during emergencies? Is your default to trust in God no matter what, or does your faith waiver when the unknown seems scary and overwhelming? It is the expression of faith in everyday life that speaks.

5. In purity. Finally, as a young person, you can expect to find listeners for what you have to say as you live a pure life before God. While this purity can be displayed in a variety of ways, I believe the biggest challenge culturally for young people is living out sexuality in a godly way. We don't know about Timothy's marital status, but we do know that he was a young man living in the sex-charged world of the first century in Ephesus, the hometown of the Diana cult. Here are some questions that both he and every young leader should answer: Will you keep far from places where you are tempted to lust? Will you live out all relationships with those of the opposite sex according to biblical standards? If you are dating, will you be devoted to abstaining from sex until you are married, and will you even avoid all appearances of impropriety? If you are married, will you honor your spouse and save all intimacy (not just physical, but also emotional and conversational) for them alone? Prayerfully consider these questions and commit yourself to the godly purity each represents, for people simply won't listen to an impure person speaking on God's behalf.

King David: The Older Generation

Psalm 71 hints at an older author ("even to old age and gray hairs," v. 18). Since there is no mention of the author's name, we can't be sure who penned this song, but many scholars attribute it to David, and it sounds like the sort of reflective prayer he would have written.

If this is David, we can imagine him in the cold marble palace during the Jerusalem winter. Crackling fire pots and the pattering of rain on the terrace lend ambience as he wraps his robe closely to ease the chill. His body is tired now. His gray and thinning hair marks well the years of running, warring and leading the people of God. Still, his mind is sharp and his soul is in a reflective mood. He summons a servant to bring him a small harp, and he begins to speak in song. And it is in this song that we learn what those old in age are uniquely qualified to speak on God's behalf.

"My mouth is filled with your praise, / and with your glory all the day" (Psalm 71:8). An older generation has a unique voice of praise within the fellowship of believers. Why? Well, let's consider the physical realities of old age in general. In old age, David could no longer ride into battle. He no longer danced in front of the multitudes as he had when the ark entered Jerusalem (2 Samuel 6:14). Frankly, he spent most of his time napping, enjoying the view of the Kidron Valley from his palace, sharing meals with his family and working on blueprints for the temple. At the end of life, activities tend to slow, and this slowing allows one to enjoy a different awareness of God.

Often, in our younger years, the pace of life is so fast that we have to work to squeeze in prayer time here, some Scripture reading there and a reflective moment whenever we can. In old age, however, the schedule is less hectic, and there is more time for focusing on God. Yes, I realize this is not necessarily true for all older people. Some are still incredibly active, but the physical fact remains that the body slows down, allowing us to take in more sunsets, smell more roses, watch more birds and marvel at more summer storms. All of these quiet moments lend themselves to plenty of praise. An older generation may have the greatest of opportunities in the winter of life to speak more praise to God, because they observe him more.

"My mouth will tell of your righteous acts, / of your deeds of salvation all the day" (Psalm 71:15). Another reality for David as he praised and reflected on God was that he began to reminisce about his journey and to recall many instances in which God had miraculously saved him and his people. Surely David never forgot the day God delivered Goliath into the hands of the young shepherd boy. Surely he recalled a few battle scenes when all seemed lost, but somehow God delivered him. He may have recalled the shame of fleeing Jerusalem because of his son's rebellion and how God had returned him to his throne. In short, God had been faithful.

An older generation in Christ has the greatest opportunity to speak of God's righteous acts and deeds of salvation simply because they have experienced more of them. Beginning with their personal story of coming to faith in Jesus, an older generation can proclaim many answered prayers, strength through struggles and times when God miraculously intervened.

Be intentional with this; write down the victories that God brought about in your life. Journal about your memories of the crucial moments when God was most obvious to you. Begin with your family. Make sure they know the story of God's righteous acts throughout your life. As God opens doors, make sure you share what only you can share: a lifetime of God's unique faithfulness toward you.

"So even to old age and gray hairs, / O God, do not forsake me, / until I proclaim your might to another generation" (Psalm 71:18). Perhaps David could see the inevitable end. He was aware that eventually he would die and that he was closer than ever to that reality. But he wanted to hang on long enough

to proclaim God to another generation. Maybe he was thinking of his son Solomon who soon would sit on his throne. Perhaps he wanted to give one more majestic speech to the people of Jerusalem. The Hebrew word translated here as *proclaim* (*nagad*) indicates something that is done in public. Was this indicating his desire to speak before the Israelites on an upcoming feast day, or was he just articulating a final prayer of blessing (see 1 Chronicles 29:20)? We are not sure what all the psalmist intended when he asked God to let him speak to another generation, but we know he desired to pass it on to the people of God who would come after him.

As an older person in the church, I encourage those of you in my generation to engage younger generations in conversation. The faith that resides currently in every Christian since the beginning of the church is built on the faith of older generations who proclaimed God's might to those who came behind them. And this might be a surprise: young people in the church really do want to hear how God has worked in your life, and you have so much to share. You may not be sought after for some leadership roles that younger leaders have now assumed, but you have something they don't. You can speak of God's faithfulness to all generations, and there may not be a more important voice.

One last word: setting an example and proclaiming God's goodness is not limited to any age categories. You're never too old to speak by making an impression, and you're never too young to praise God for his righteous acts. More than anything, find your voice. Generations may speak of God in different ways, but all generations speak.

Week Six

Devotional Readings

....

MONDAY
Youth Speak

> *Let no one despise you for your youth,*
> *but set the believers an example in speech,*
> *in conduct, in love, in faith, in purity.*

1 TIMOTHY 4:12

Believe it or not, accept it or not, I still feel nineteen even though I have long passed my teenage years. I'm now in my sixth decade of life but continue to think of myself as young at heart. What I recall about those earlier years is the burning desire that I had to be a genuine apprentice to Jesus. After a couple of prodigal-like years, I came to place my trust in him, just as Timothy did. Again, we don't exactly know how old he was. He was young enough to need Paul's sobering reminder about how to live an exemplary life and old enough to want to speak up for Jesus and be heard.

So, consider with me one more time the five ways Timothy and young people in general can find their youthful voice in a pagan culture. First, be an example in speech. Monitor your small talk daily. Are you words true, helpful, inspiring, necessary and kind? Second, be an example in conduct. How we live our everyday lives either draws others toward Jesus or distracts others from him. Third, be an example in love. Genuine love is hard to refute. Look for practical ways to show Jesus' love today. Fourth, be an example in faith. Be a doer of the Word. Fifth and finally, be an example in purity. Stick to God's standards, not the world's.

Youth speak. That's a given. Being heard or not heard depends on our attachment to Jesus.

Week Six

TUESDAY
Elderly Speak

> *So even to old age and gray hairs,*
> *O God, do not forsake me,*
> *until I proclaim your might to another generation,*
> *your power to all those to come.*

PSALM 71:18

I'm getting older and will someday be old. So will you. No one escapes the curse of sin and death. That's the bad news. Now for the good news. Psalm 71:18 is a reminder to all generations, especially the elderly, that God has a plan that enables all of us to partner with him in sharing his story. There are no age limits, no retirement dates. The writer of this psalm has lived long enough to conclude that God can be trusted and praised. He wants future generations to know what he has discovered about the Maker of heaven and earth.

One of my heroes of faith is George Müller (1805–1898), the founder of the famous Bristol, England, orphanages. He cared for and raised some ten thousand orphans during his lifetime. Time and space do not permit the recording of all that he did for children in the name of Jesus. All of that is noteworthy, but even more extraordinary is what happened in his later years. As a young man, he longed to enter global missions. Not until he was seventy did he begin a distinguished seventeen-year season of missionary travel. Did you catch that? At *seventy* he took on a new passion for sharing the good news of Jesus Christ. Those who heard him often commented on the youthful vigor and passion with which he spoke.

The elderly have an advantage over many of us. They have the privilege of a long view. Like the psalmist, from youth to old age, they have witnessed God's faithfulness in good times and bad times. Please keep speaking, elderly brother or sister. We are listening.

Week Six

WEDNESDAY
Children Speak

But when the chief priests and the scribes saw the wonderful
things that he did, and the children crying out in the temple,
"Hosanna to the Son of David!" they were indignant.

MATTHEW 21:15

The religious leaders of Jesus' day did not like the fact that children were shouting praises to him. The Scriptures tell us they were indignant. The Greek word translated *indignant* is an old word that originally brought together two words: *much* and *grieve*. I'm sure you get the picture. The term was often used to describe physical pain. Matthew 21:15 uses *indignant* to tell us how greatly annoyed the priests and scribes were with the hosannas coming from the lips of children for Jesus. *Hosanna* comes from a Hebrew word that means "save, please!" In the Gospels, *hosanna* is used as a shout of joy recognizing that salvation has come. The old saying "Children should be seen and not heard" must have been a favorite of these dour leaders.

Children have a knack for saying things that the rest of us are thinking. Years ago, while I was preaching, my oldest daughter, seated on my wife's lap, cried out, "Daddy, my buns hurt." (She said some other things too that I won't repeat in this devotional reflection.) My sermon had gone way too long. Everyone was thinking it; she said it. After the laughter died down, I prayed, and that was that. Children speak.

During my years as a Jesus-follower, I have watched with absolute amazement at the number of times children said the most remarkable things at just the right time in just the right way. I know there are those embarrassing moments when we wish they were silent. However, God—the great Designer— intended for them to speak their hearts. It is a beautiful thing when they speak of Jesus. *not minds*

Week Six

THURSDAY
Babies Speak

And they said to him, "Do you hear what these are saying?"
And Jesus said to them, "Yes; have you never read,
'Out of the mouth of infants and nursing
babies you have prepared praise?'"

MATTHEW 21:16

Jesus is having an edgy conversation with the religious leaders somewhere on the temple grounds. These are the same bitter leaders we talked about in Wednesday's devotional. Jesus' reply to their wanting the children to stop the hosannas is rather abrupt. He simply quotes from Psalm 8:2 and departs their company. This psalm is that magnificent song or prayer that celebrates the majestic name of God. It is a powerful reminder that every voice, every life is designed by God to give him praise, even the most marginalized and insignificant. Helpless infants cannot be silenced.

I'm a grandfather who delights in holding his grandchildren. If the oldest one continues to grow, he will eventually hold me! I cherish the memories of cooing babies and nursing infants. I delight in praying over them and singing to them, though I'm not very good at the latter. Even the routine burp and sometimes volcanic spit-up have not lessened my love. I have lost

several expensive ties while coaxing the resistant burp from
one of the kids. (I never liked those ties anyway.) I know about
dirty diapers, and I have a graduate degree in sleepless nights.
Infants are full-time employers. They are a demanding seven
pounds and eight ounces of constant need.

Most of us don't think of babies as speakers of God's great
narrative, but Jesus would disagree with us. He heard the
gurgles and the giggles as sounds of praise to their Creator.
Babies speak. The wise listen.

reagan has already influenced my
decisions and behaviors.

Week Six

FRIDAY
All Generations Speak

> *For behold, from now on all generations*
> *will call me blessed.*
>
> LUKE 1:48

A llow me to set the record straight humbly. Mary was not self-promoting when she spoke these words of praise that we now call "The Magnificat." She was exalting God for his divine rescue operation in and through the incarnation. She was anticipating and celebrating the birth of Zechariah and Elizabeth's baby, John, the forerunner of Jesus. But this unlikely candidate in God's story also knew that she would give birth to the Son of God (Luke 1:35). Mary would be the conduit through which God in flesh would be born. Born of a virgin. Born of a poor teenager. Born of an uneducated mother with no résumé, no power and no fame. Mary's only qualification was her faith in the God who makes the impossible possible. All God-aware generations would join her in praising God as Savior and Redeemer.

Generations is the word *genea* in the Greek New Testament. The term can refer to a race of people, a particular people in a specific time or successive people of various ages who live during the same time. People today usually think of a generation as something that comprises a given age group. What must be retold is the story, the grand narrative that reveals just how much God loves the world, this place fractured by sin and marred by death. God had a plan that included an unwed virgin, a confused fiancé, a host of angels, a sleepy village, searching magi, hardworking shepherds, a bewildered innkeeper, a jealous king, an unaware planet, male and female, rich and poor, powerful and powerless, and finally, you and me. Who will speak of that?

seven

We Will Never
Stop Speaking

According to government records, the late and longtime South Carolina senator Strom Thurmond took his place behind the podium on the Senate floor at 8:54 p.m. on August 28, 1957. The bill in question was the Civil Rights Act of 1957, and the debate was heated from both sides of the aisle. On this occasion, Thurmond decided to use the political strategy of debate called a filibuster. Since the inception of our government, lawmakers have used filibusters when they are opposed to a bill in question and the direction they see the vote going. The goal is to take advantage of their turn at the podium by speaking until the bill in question is stalled, prevented or removed. It rarely changes the outcome, yet lawmakers continue to employ this method.

On this occasion, Thurmond did not stop speaking until 9:12 p.m. the following evening. His speech included everything he could possibly think of. Transcripts show that his talk included "the reciting of Declaration of Independence, Bill of Rights, President George Washington's farewell address and other historical documents along the way."[1] All told, he spoke for twenty-four hours and eighteen minutes, the longest filibuster speech ever given in the US Senate. But he was not alone. Several other senators teamed up with Thurmond to filibuster for fifty-seven straight days, speaking virtually nonstop from March 26 to June 19, the date on which the bill was actually voted on and passed into law in spite of their effort.

Most of us could never imagine talking for this long, especially about nothing in particular. But what if the words of the speech really mattered? What if the speakers were not stalling or spouting rehearsed political lines? What if the message was one of good news concerning life and death for all people? And what if all the talkers was truly and passionately convinced that their testimony was true? This is how our first-century, early church brothers and sisters understood their speaking. Their question was not how they could keep talking, but how they could stop.

The Early Church Speaks

In chapter 1 we discovered that because of the truth that Christians have experienced, they can't help but speak. But as the story of the early church continues, the Bible also reveals that they were committed to speaking this truth on an ongoing basis. Luke the physician reveals this commitment when he writes, "And every day, in the temple and from house to house, they did not cease teaching and preaching that the Christ is Jesus" (Acts 5:42). Early on the church refused to silence the truth, but as it grew it remained committed to speaking this truth constantly, consistently and continuously. They could not help it, and they could not stop it. It still hasn't stopped. The church started speaking then, and it is still speaking to this day. In other words, the testimony, witness, defense, teaching and preaching of the Word by the church in the world is a two-thousand-year-old speech that hasn't ended.

In Acts 5 we are given access to a story that displays the resolve of early Christians to keep speaking, and once again we find it was born out of intense persecution. By this time the church had an average weekly attendance of over five thousand (Acts 4:4), and this rapid growth continued: "And more than ever believers were added to the Lord, multitudes of both men and women" (5:14). In a few short years, Christianity had become the dominant religious force in Jerusalem. But this fueled the jealously of the Jewish religious leaders (see 5:17), so during a church worship service on Solomon's Portico, they had the leaders of the movement arrested and the twelve apostles were put in the public jail.

I wish we could have had priority backstage passes to the holy company and conversation in the jail cell that night. Did they pray? Did they reminisce about experiences they had when Jesus walked with them? Did they encourage one another? Did they sing hymns? Was Matthew working on his gospel? I suppose we won't be able to answer these questions until we get to heaven, but whatever took place, it didn't last long. "During the night an angel of the Lord opened the prison doors and brought them out." What did the angel tell them to do? "Go and stand in the temple and speak to the people all the words of this Life" (5:19).

Well, the next morning, when the high priest and the Jewish council sent for the Twelve to interrogate them, the soldiers found an empty jail cell. Puzzled and confused, they wondered how this would all turn out. Suddenly someone rushed into the assembly to report that the fugitives in question were preaching again in the temple courts. The officers were sent again, but this time they didn't arrest the apostles; they simply invited them to come of their own volition. Looking for another opportunity to speak on behalf of their Lord, these men willingly returned to the Jewish leaders.

Nothing had really changed since the last time they'd found themselves before those religious men, on trial before the sacred assembly. Same question: Why are you still preaching about Jesus? Same answer: We have to do what God tells us to do. Same result: the Pharisees and Sadducees flipped and wanted to kill them! Same debate: What are we gonna do with these guys? Same persecution: "And when they had called in the apostles, they beat them and charged them not to speak in the name of Jesus, and let them go" (Acts 5:40). Same result: they didn't stop talking about Jesus.

Before we get to our challenge to "never stop speaking," let's dig into the punishment in this story. They "beat them" is the Greek word *derō* that means to "flay or skin,"[2] which gives you an idea of what the apostles' backs looked like after the beating. They were likely beaten according to Jewish law with thirty-nine strikes, usually administered with rods. (Forty was the limit, and they usually stopped one short; see Deuteronomy 25:3.) This would have left them with bleeding wounds, torn skin and deep bruising. It would be the first of many beatings these men would endure in the name of Christ.

This causes us to consider what punishment or persecution we might receive for speaking about Jesus. In other words, just how dangerous is it for us to speak? Seriously, wrestle with the question: what's the worst thing that could happen to me if I refuse to quit speaking for Jesus? May these fearless Christ-followers inspire us to have the same courageous faith.

This, then, is the lesson: these early church leaders had a

choice to make. They had been charged "not to speak in the name of Jesus" (Acts 5:40), but the angel of the Lord told them, "Go . . . speak to the people all the words of this Life" (5:20). If they chose to speak as God had commanded them, they would be punished. If they remained silent, they could avoid persecution, but not do God's will. You and I also have the same choice to make. Will we speak continually on behalf of Jesus as his witnesses, or will we let the world shut us up? As for the apostles, they "did not cease" to speak (5:42). *never let them have that power*

The word combination used in the original language of this text may give us a deeper understanding of our call to keep speaking. Using the English "not cease" is a correct representation of the original words (*ou pauō*). But understanding that the root of this word means "to pause"[3] may provide a clearer metaphor of our call to share the good news all the time. Microwave ovens, DVRs, video games and the videos we download onto our iPads and iPhones are all controlled simply with three buttons: Play, Stop, and Pause. When we're ready to watch or microwave or play, we push Play, and when we are finished we push Stop. But if we are interrupted, we simply push Pause.

This is a simple picture of how the early church saw their call to share their faith. If we symbolically see our witness as a spiritual smartphone, there is only one button. By the grace of Jesus, our faith pushes Play, and by his Spirit we live out God's purpose and calling for our lives. We've learned that there is no Stop, because we can't help speaking of this great gift. But this verse reminds us that there is no Pause. You could paraphrase Acts 5:42 "they never pushed the Pause button on the teaching and preaching about Jesus." What does it look like if we never push Pause in our witness?

Teaching and Preaching

First, we note exactly what they didn't cease from. There are two kinds of speaking listed in Acts 5:42. The first is teaching, and this word in the original language has to do with a formal kind of discourse or instruction in which someone is dispensing information to another. Of course, the apostles were the authoritative voices of instruction in the early church. In fact, their teaching became one of four things that marked the early community of believers (see Acts 2:42). And certainly this verse means that the apostles (who had just been beaten for speaking) continued to teach and instruct in the ways of Christ. But it wasn't limited to them.

Christianity quickly became a movement in which everyone was entrusted with some leadership responsibilities. The apostles simply couldn't teach all of the lessons, so we can guess that they entrusted teaching to others, as Paul encourages Timothy to do: "What you have heard from me in the presence of many witnesses entrust to faithful men who will be able to teach others also" (2 Timothy 2:2). This is in addition to the in-home teaching that was so much of the Hebrew culture and surely migrated its way into the Christian Jewish family curriculum.

The implication is that every Christian is a teacher. This is not to say that there are not gifted teachers who assume teaching leadership roles within the church, but just an observation that (on some level) in Jesus we all become teachers. Even the newest of Christians have some knowledge and information concerning the faith that they can share with others. Often this is a simple explanation of faith with some diagrams about salvation and a few Scriptures memorized, but it is instruction nonetheless.

Through the years, I have also been reminded that my best learning comes from my responsibility to teach. I believe this is true of thousands of Christians weekly as small group leaders, Sunday school teachers, children's ministry workers and youth sponsors who teach truths they learned in preparation. And in the same way the early church did, parents are responsible for teaching the faith to their family.

It may be helpful to think about the people in your life you teach or have taught. Don't push Pause. Keep teaching.

And keep preaching. Now, if you were intimidated by the encouragement to teach, the challenge to preach will likely push you over the edge. But don't jump to conclusions quite yet. I'm not talking about getting up in front of a bunch of people on Sunday morning and standing behind a pulpit. That, of course, is preaching as we have come to know it, and some do it in an official capacity. But the word used in Acts 5:42, *euangelizō*, is more encompassing because it simply means to tell good news. This is the job of preachers—both those who stand in the pulpit and those who stand in every corner of our culture. Believe or not, you are called to preach. Preaching simply entails telling the good news and this comes naturally for us all; we speak good news. The key is to not stop.

Every Day

This leads us to the when of this preaching and teaching. Our verse teaches us that they preached and taught every day of the week. There were no days off for the apostles or the church. They didn't limit their speaking to Sunday; they were at it every day. We don't know exactly what form this daily teaching took, but we do know that there was a lot to talk about. Thousands were learning to connect Old Testament teachings about the Christ (Messiah) to Jesus and to see him as the fulfillment of those prophecies. Some were discovering what this new covenant meant for their relationship with God. Outsiders were still inquiring about the Holy Spirit and what had taken place thus far in the church. In other words, there was much to teach and preach. They simply did it every day.

From the example of our first-century brothers and sisters, we may be inspired to speak every day. Of course, we are called to hear sermons and lessons on Sunday from preachers and teachers when the whole church gathers together, but for the Christ-follower, every day becomes a day of speaking on behalf of Jesus. Literally every day becomes the right time to share your faith with those around you.

But you'll have to cultivate a holy desire for these conversations. It may be helpful to begin with a daily prayer inviting God into every conversation. In this way, you are revealing a willingness to speak for God and a reliance on him to open the door. After this, you can go about your daily routine with sensitivity to the Holy Spirit's movement in the lives of those around you and simply respond as he leads.

Everywhere

With this prayer and this godly intention in place, virtually every place in this world can become a place where you teach and preach. The passage we have been studying reveals that they continued speaking in two specific locations. One of them was the most public of Jewish places in the first century—the temple. This likely is a reference to what seemed to be their general corporate worship location at Solomon's Portico (Acts 5:12). But they also met from house to house. Considering the size of Jerusalem in the first century (about twenty thousand residents) and the number of believers, it is likely that you couldn't find a neighborhood in town that wasn't hosting a Christian house meeting. In other words, the early church was meeting every day, and they were meeting everywhere.

Again, inspired by this widespread coverage, we should view every location as a potential place for speaking the good news of Jesus. It could be a conversation standing in line at the coffee shop early in the morning, in the hallway of school between classes or in the bleachers during a youth soccer match.

In addition to the numerous homes that host small group Bible studies each week all across the country, virtually anywhere we find ourselves can be a place for sharing what we know about Jesus and for declaring the good news. The goal is to provide a never-ceasing voice to this culture, to literally cover every place in each community with the teaching and preaching that the Christ is Jesus.

The cool thing is that we are called to never stop speaking, and by God's design we never will. As the old hymn says, "And when in scenes of glory I sing a new, new song, / 'Twill be the old, old story that I have loved so long. / I love to tell the story." The story we tell is a story that lasts. It's the only one that matters. This message is truth in an age of talk. And this message has been entrusted to us.

So we'll never stop speaking about it.

ask them what
they think about
God and faith—
instead of focusing on
"well this is what I believe"...

Week Seven

Devotional Readings

....

MONDAY
We Will Never Stop Speaking

> *And every day, in the temple and from house to*
> *house, they did not cease teaching and*
> *preaching that the Christ is Jesus.*
>
> **ACTS 5:42**

[handwritten marginalia: was it easier for them because they knew him? they should that be our prayer?]

C all it whatever you want—persistence, faithfulness, determination, endurance or stick-to-itiveness—these early Jesus-followers had it in full measure. They did not stop talking about Jesus. The specific language in Acts 5:42 has fascinated me for a long time. I might paraphrase the verse like this: "All through the day, every single day, these apprentices to Jesus did nothing but talk about him in the very place they had been arrested earlier and in houses all over Jerusalem. These disciples simply kept up the same conversation and the same topic of Jesus and Jesus alone. They went into microteaching and macropreaching by reminding their audience that Jesus is God's promised good news!" Unstoppable!

What does that really look like in today's world? In 2014 I was profoundly privileged to travel with our pastoral leadership team to India. Specifically, we went to teach and preach Jesus at a conference hosted by Central India Christian Mission and Dr. Ajai Lall. Some six hundred preachers had traveled far and wide to be fed spiritually and encouraged. Paradoxically we were the ones nurtured and blessed.

One afternoon, through translators, we heard testimonies of persecution that included torture, rape and murder for many who dared to speak of Jesus. It was one of the most delightful and most difficult conversations I have ever encountered. We cried, prayed and encouraged one another to never stop speaking of Jesus.

What about you? Is your mind made up? Is your heart resolved? Call it whatever you want: silly, suicidal or strategic.

Week Seven

TUESDAY
Power to Speak

But you will receive power when the Holy Spirit has come upon you, and you will be my witnesses in Jerusalem and in all Judea and Samaria, and to the end of the earth.

ACTS 1:8

We are a power-obsessed world. Some devote time to the pursuit of political punch. Some are preoccupied with the military kind. Still others make their life's objective one of financial, educational or personal strength. The early disciples were not preoccupied with any of that kind of power. Jesus had chosen them. Three-plus years had come and gone in their extensive apprenticeship with him. They had walked, watched and wondered at his remarkable life. They had witnessed his miracles, experienced his love and been eyewitnesses to his death, burial and resurrection.

The world-sized commission to speak of him everywhere was to begin. This global undertaking could be fulfilled only with the might and power of the Holy Spirit. Spiritual assignments can be accomplished only with spiritual resources. The worldwide mission of the church can be carried out only with the immeasurable size of the Holy Spirit.

The promise of Acts 1:8 was fulfilled on the day of Pentecost.

The Spirit that empowered Jesus is the same Spirit that empowers us. Now and then we get a glimpse of what this power looks like. I believe that when we dare to speak of Jesus, especially to those who don't know him yet, the Spirit is at work. He is at work awakening slumbering hearts to receive this free gift of forgiveness and restoration in and through Jesus.

I don't have the power to change someone else's life, and neither do you. We speak to an unsaved friend at our favorite coffee shop or to an unbelieving coworker at the office water fountain by *his* power.

Week Seven

WEDNESDAY
A Prayer to Speak

And now, Lord, look upon their threats and grant to your
servants to continue to speak your word with all boldness.

ACTS 4:29

P eter and John had defied the threats of the Sanhedrin. A
night in jail was their punishment. Summoned to appear
before the authorities, these two witnesses of Jesus' death,
burial and resurrection took their stand. They listened cor-
dially and were charged "not to speak or teach at all in the
name of Jesus" (Acts 4:18). However, Peter and John had
made up their minds while incarcerated. They were resolved
to go on speaking of Jesus.

The authorities released them, and these two disciples returned to their friends and reported what the religious leaders
had said. What followed was a spontaneous prayer meeting.

Anyone can talk big and bold. The real proof rests in following through with action. God has given me numerous opportunities to speak on his behalf. I have failed more than I
have succeeded. Still, time and time again, God brings holy
appointments my way. I cherish those moments when, in
boldness, I speak of him.

I had one of those encounters not long ago. A man was
holding one of those "homeless" signs that have become all too

common. I prayed for boldness, bought him some food, got out of my car and entered into a sweet time of conversation. I listened to his troubling story. I spoke to him of the hope that is only found in Christ. He shared his burden, and I shared my story. He spoke of addictions, and I spoke of my Savior.

My task is not conversion. That's God's. My task is to speak the story with all boldness. I keep praying along with Peter and John. I trust you do too.

asia
africa
europe

Week Seven

THURSDAY
God Provides the Fruit

And the word of God continued to increase, and the number
of the disciples multiplied greatly in Jerusalem, and a great
many of the priests became obedient to the faith.

ACTS 6:7

The church of Jerusalem gradually and continually grew.
Those early apprentices to Jesus simply kept on speaking of
their Lord and Savior. Dr. Luke, the writer of Acts, was so capti-
vated by this supernatural growth, he inserted six summary
statements throughout his account of the Holy Spirit's work
through the life of the early church. Acts 6:7 is one of those sum-
maries. (See also Acts 2:47; 9:31; 12:24; 16:5; 19:20.) These faithful
witnesses to Jesus spoke, and God produced. Nothing stopped
them: not early birth pains, not opposition, not prejudice, not
disagreement, not rejection and not personal threats. What does
it take to stop us from speaking of Jesus?

Most of us live in a time and place where persecution
doesn't come in the form of bodily harm. Some of us know
the sting of rejection. We know what it is like to be mocked
or marginalized. Few of us, though, experience the kind of
persecution that these first Jesus-followers did. What, then,
does it take to stop us from speaking of Jesus?

I'm getting older, and will one day be old, if Jesus tarries and he gives me good health. I want my life marked—completely and totally labeled—with that of being a faithful Jesus-follower. The lesson that God is teaching me, and he is persistent in this, is that *he* produces when I speak. His fruit is the eternal kind. Men, women and children introduced to Jesus, saved by Jesus and matured in Jesus is the result. Speak. God will produce.

Week Seven

FRIDAY
Persuading Speech

> *"King Agrippa, do you believe the prophets? I know that you believe." And Agrippa said to Paul, "In a short time would you persuade me to be a Christian?" And Paul said, "Whether short or long, I would to God that not only you but also all who hear me this day might become such as I am—except for these chains."*

> ACTS 26:27-29

I admire Paul more than I can possibly express. His conversion to Christ on the Damascus Road forever altered his view of life. From that day forward, he saturated everything and everyone with the good news of Jesus. Paul was compelled to speak of the Jesus he had met on that dusty Syrian highway. This apostle told anyone who would listen about what Christ had done for him. He spoke of Jesus' life and ministry, his death and resurrection, and his promise and gift of eternal life. He was persuasive. The word *persuaded* (*peithō*) means to be convinced, won over or experience a change of mind. King Agrippa, a would-be powerbroker ruling over a small sliver of Roman real estate now called Lebanon was no match for God's spokesman.

Where does persuasive gospel-speech find its source? The answer is simple. When people meet Jesus and become convinced that he is the sovereign Lord of the universe, they are forever incapable of keeping it to themselves.

This book is not some full-court press to get the reluctant to testify to Jesus. It is a simple reminder of the marriage that took place between his story and our story. Anyone forgiven much will speak much. We speak every day and everywhere because we are persuaded by his love.

Discussion Guide

How to Use This Discussion Guide

Thank you for your willingness to participate in this study. We pray that this material will work its way into the lives of thousands of participants in hundreds of small groups. This study is designed to synthesize a variety of resources in various venues. Over the next seven weeks, you will experience

- daily reading for personal reflection,
- weekly video teachings and discussions for group interaction and shared insights,
- occasional action points to help mobilize groups and individuals toward application, and
- weekend church services that reinforce the weekly themes (if you are studying this material with your whole church community).

To get the most out of this study, commit to the daily readings and review each week's discussion guide prior to meeting as a group. Here you'll see each week's discussion framed by four main sections:

- *Gather.* Whether establishing environments for new groups or deepening relationships with existing group members, this segment is designed to accentuate what it means to gather together.

- *Grow.* In this segment of the discussion, there will be ample opportunities to examine the ways in which the stories from Scripture intersect with the stories of group members. Here you will broaden and deepen biblical insights together. The DVD segments will enhance your conversation.

- *Give.* This section of the study is intended to empower you and your group to take action, ministering to the group and through the group. Here you will engage in practices that turn reflections into actions.

- *Go.* If the "Give" section is about serving, the "Go" section is about mission. This segment will point group participants toward reaching beyond the members and toward the mission field around them.

A student ministries guide through this material is available for free download at eastviewchurch.net/wespeak.

We are confident that God will use this resource to help you "proclaim truth in an age of talk." Your thoughtful participation within the group discussions and between the meetings will help you to maximize this resource. Together, we speak.

Jim Probst

Week
One

We Cannot Help But Speak

Gather

Our theme for this week is "we cannot help but speak," but one of the greatest challenges for many of us is overcoming our fear of speaking in a group discussion. Let's resolve this fear right away. First, you don't need to be a Bible scholar to contribute to this study. The daily reading will help you to stay on track, and the discussion guide will help you to anticipate where the conversation is going. Take a moment to prepare an answer to a simple discussion starter below, and look for opportunities to contribute throughout the discussion. Your honest insights and questions will help the group more than you know.

- For newly formed groups: Describe a team, group or organization that you've enjoyed in the past. What made it so special?

- For preexisting groups: If you had to give a five-minute impromptu speech, what topic would you choose? Why?

Grow

1. Invite someone in the group to begin the study by leading the group in prayer.

2. Watch the video for week 1, "We Cannot Help But Speak." Add to the following highlights as you note insightful or important comments.

   - "In other words, when God speaks, nothing is ever the same again. As a matter of fact, we have an Old Testament book called Deuteronomy, and the Hebrew word is the plural of this word *dabar*. . . . From the word *dabar* comes that image of God drawing his people into himself, putting his mighty hands on their face and communicating his heart to their heart." J. K. Jones

   - "We speak because God has spoken. God is a talker, and from Genesis 1:3, 'Let there be light,' his creative words and powerful word have been speaking throughout human history." Mike Baker

   - "Abraham now is our example for obeying and going, and the encouragement this week is that you will say, 'God, if you're sending me somewhere—if you're sending me to the classroom, to the gym, down the street, the cubicle next to me—wherever you're sending me, I will go and I will speak on your behalf.' That's what *We Speak* is all about." Mike Baker

3. Did anything surprise or inspire you in this week's video? Explain.

4. We can summarize Genesis 12:1-4 by saying that God has spoken (*dabar*) and that he has specifically spoken a blessing over Abraham. As a group, take a moment to

share at least ten obvious areas of your lives where God has demonstrated his "blessings."

5. God blesses us in order to bless others through us. In what ways are people tempted to hoard God's blessings rather than distribute them?

6. Referencing Acts 4:20, J. K. wrote, "Peter and John, followers of Jesus, were charged not to speak. They were threatened with the promise that if they continued to talk, harm would befall them. Yet they kept speaking of Jesus. There was no wiggle room in their worldview. They had to talk about him. He was their grand subject. His life was their glorious sermon. Can that be recovered in us today?" Discuss this as a group.

7. How would you have handled such hostility to the good news of God's blessings?

8. What particular comments or concepts from this week's reading captured your attention?

Give

9. In the first chapter of *We Speak*, Mike wrote, "And we have seen what God has done in each of our journeys. In other words, when people ask, we can address their questions; when they want to know about our faith, we can instruct them; and while the world is filled with bad news, we can herald the *good* news. We have seen. We have heard. We speak." Describe a situation in which you find it difficult to share your faith.

10. Take a moment to briefly speak of how God has spoken to you. Do you recall the time when you first heard his voice

through Scripture, circumstance, a sermon or a person who shared the good news with you? Explain.

11. Share prayer requests with the group, inviting someone to take notes and to email the requests to the entire group after the meeting.

Go

12. In the video teaching today, Mike said, "But here's what I know when it comes to sharing our faith in Jesus Christ; we're going to have to leave something. . . . I'm trying to talk you into sharing your faith over the next several weeks and then throughout the rest of your life." Begin praying for opportunities to speak of God's goodness to those who will listen.

13. Pray for one another as you conclude the meeting today. Pray that the group is an encouragement to one another and that there are opportunities to share hope with others between your meetings.

14. Continue reading the daily devotionals in preparation for next week's discussion and application.

Week
Two

We Speak Good News

Gather

Take a moment to prepare an answer to a simple discussion starter below and look for opportunities to contribute throughout the discussion. The discussion starter is designed to invite you to share experiences without necessarily needing the "right" answer.

- For newly formed groups: It's been said that good news travels fast. Share about an event from your past when you were eager to share some good news.

- For preexisting groups: Share a personal or family highlight, recognizing God's blessings from the past week.

Grow

1. Invite someone in the group to begin the study by leading the group in prayer, giving thanks for the highlights shared as you gathered today.

2. Watch the video for week 2, "We Speak Good News." Add to the following highlights as you note insightful or important comments.

- • "I love Scripture, and one of the words in the Hebrew Bible that gives shape to the idea of Scripture is the Hebrew word *Torah*. . . . It carries the idea of instruction or doctrine. . . . Behind that word is the significance of a relationship with God." J. K. Jones

- • "He gathered all the children of Israel together in what I've described as the most boring worship service in the history of the world. He got them on Mount Ebal and Mount Gerizim—all the people: men, women, young and old. And he read the entire book of the law of Moses—the whole Torah—because he said, 'We don't ever wanna miss this again. We wanna follow the Word of God specifically and explicitly, so that he brings victory with his people.' And so there is a lesson here for us as we speak the Word of God." Mike Baker

- • "It is a bloody book, but you know what. It's not any more bloody than the cross. And that's where I always just go right to that. And so listen, if you want to get angry at God, look at how serious sin is by the death of his Son on the cross." Mike Baker

3. Did anything surprise or inspire you in this week's video? Explain.

4. As a group, read Joshua 1:1-9 (emphasizing v. 8) and 8:34-35.

5. Joshua's story reveals great victories when following God's directions and great struggles when disregarding them. Do you think people in our culture see God's instructions as an opening or as an obstacle for daily living? Explain.

6. In chapter 2 of *We Speak*, Mike gave three reasons for our

silence in sharing the good news. First, Christians feel unqualified to share news that is so good. Second, Christians are afraid that others won't believe the good news when they share it. Third, Christians don't understand the urgency of the situation. Which of these three most accurately describes your silence from time to time? Explain.

7. In Tuesday's daily reading, J. K. noted, "Isn't that the nature of God? He takes a sin-riddled self and exchanges it for a Savior-filled purpose. When that exchange is truly grasped, who could resist speaking up for Jesus?" Do you agree? Explain.

Give

8. Email or text your group a passage such as Psalm 119:33-34 to remind one another of the way in which God's law (Torah) intersects with the good news (gospel). Discuss it, and remember to "Reply All" to keep everyone in the conversation.

9. Share prayer requests with the group, inviting someone to take notes and to forward the requests to the entire group after the meeting.

Go

10. In the video teaching today, Jim said, "In Psalm 119:33-35, we hear a prayer that reflects what we've heard today. 'Teach me, O LORD, the way of your statutes; / and I will keep it to the end. / Give me understanding, that I may keep your law / and observe it with my whole heart. / Lead me in the path of your commandments, / for I delight in it.' The action point today is to delight in the com-

mandments of God. Take time this week to audibly express the Ten Commandments in your small group and in your home. Strive to embrace the good news that we see in his commands."

11. Invite one person to read Exodus 20:1-17 aloud for the group.

12. Conclude your meeting by praying together as a group.

13. Continue reading the daily devotionals in preparation for next week's discussion and application.

We Speak Even If
No One Listens

Gather

As your group gathers today, take advantage of this discussion starter. For some, this is the opportunity to contribute to discussion verbally, regardless of their level of biblical knowledge.

- In what size of group do you feel most effective or comfortable in communicating? Explain.

- Describe the time when you were most nervous speaking in front of a group? Was it due to the size, the content of the message, the context or something else?

Grow

1. Invite someone in the group to begin the study by leading the group in prayer, thanking the King who listens to his servants as they pray.

2. Watch the video for week 3, "We Speak Even If No One Listens." Add to the following highlights as you note insightful or important comments.

   • "*Navi*ʾ is the word that we're studying today. It's a Hebrew word. It's a word that gets translated in our Bibles [as] *prophet*. It literally means 'one who bubbles over' or 'bubbles up.' It's a picture of the prophet's proximity to God—where God would pour his message into that servant and that servant then would speak forth what God had placed there." J. K. Jones

   • "One of the biggest challenges for us as we speak on behalf of God is that we're just afraid to go. We're afraid to go give the message that God wants us to give. We're afraid of the reaction of the people. And I just want to encourage you: if God's love really is bubbling up from your heart, then you and I are called to go." Mike Baker

   • "This is an incredible story! Jonah goes finally and does what God tells him to do. He preaches this great sermon. Everybody . . . changes their life, turns to God, and Jonah's not happy about it. What we find out about Jonah the prophet is that his heart is not right." Mike Baker

3. Did you take any additional notes during the video this week? What did you find helpful?

4. If *navi*ʾ communicates a "bubbling over" from the heart of the prophet to the mouth of the prophet, how did Jonah's heart/speech change throughout this story (see Jonah 1:12; 2:9; 3:4-5; 4:8-11)?

5. In Ezekiel 2:7, God told his prophet, "And you shall speak my words to them, whether they hear or refuse to hear" (see

Monday's reading for more detail). Describe a situation when you were compelled to share truth with someone, even if he or she did not express any interest in listening.

6. Has there been a season in your life when you were less likely to listen to good advice from those around you? Explain.

7. It has been said that Christians are responsible to *share* the good news, not to *guarantee* how people will respond to the good news. Do you agree?

8. What are the greatest challenges you face as you think about speaking for God (nobody's listening, no idea what to say, countercultural message, not an eloquent speaker, etc.)?

Give

9. In Tuesday's reading, J. K. noted, "Being a Jesus-follower gives us no guarantee that we will always understand the prompting voice of God. This very day he could call us to speak of Jesus to our resistant neighbor. This very day he might orchestrate a divine appointment of sharing good news with a total stranger at our local Walmart....We speak even when it doesn't make sense. Stay alert." In what ways are you staying alert and available to speak on God's behalf?

10. Is there a Scripture reference that is "bubbling over" in your life right now? If so, use this time to share the passage with the group to encourage their faith.

Go

11. At the conclusion of the video teaching today, we heard Matthew 12:34, which reads, "For out of the abundance of the heart the mouth speaks." In light of this passage, take

time this week to conduct a "speech audit" to expose the issues that are bubbling over from your heart to your mouth. Journal at the end of each day to reflect on what you've discovered.

12. Conclude your group meeting by praying together as a group.

13. Continue reading the daily devotionals in preparation for next week's discussion and application.

We Speak Powerfully in Weakness

Gather

Utilize one of these discussion starters to engage one another in conversation, learn more about one another and establish the theme for the discussion. Today we'll be speaking of God's strength on display in our weakness.

• Briefly establish a list of occupations represented in the group. Of those listed, which would you be least qualified to do for an occupation?

• At what age were you—or would you expect to be—most physically fit?

Grow

1. Invite the group to begin the study by praying together. Consider creatively engaging the group members in prayer by having them read Scripture references that recognize God's strength (see, for example, 2 Samuel

22:32-33; Psalm 28:7; 37:39; 73:26; Luke 1:49).

2. Watch the video for week 4, "We Speak Powerfully in Weakness." Add to the following highlights as you note insightful or important comments.

- "I was in a conversation a number of years ago with a young boy, six or seven years old, and I was trying to explain nearly the unexplainable about how God can put on flesh. And the little boy listened for a while and finally said, 'Preacher, are you saying that God put on skin?' I said, 'That's it.'" J. K. Jones

- "And this is just this incredible notion that God would take his powerful word . . . every word that he has for us to live by, and to know his truth, and he would place it in the most fragile thing: a human life. And that is the reality of Jesus Christ: fully God and fully human—the power of God and yet in the fragile condition of humanity. And so, what we have here in Jesus Christ is the full expression of everything that you and I study . . . everything that you and I are trying to become in Jesus Christ as we speak." Mike Baker

- "Listen. My good friend, Tim Harlow, he's got this quote, . . . 'We need to be God's witnesses, not God's lawyer.' And the idea is that we don't have to defend Jesus. We don't have to explain Jesus. All we have to do is witness to what Jesus has done in our lives and the new life that he's given us because of his death, burial and resurrection." Mike Baker

3. Did you take any additional notes during the video this week? What did you find helpful?

4. As a group, read John 1:1-18. In this passage, you will see that the Greek word *logos* in verses 1 and 14 is translated as "Word" in the English Standard Version. What do we learn about the Word, Jesus, in this passage?

5. This same Logos (Jesus) came to earth through a first-time parent in a humble manger (see Luke 2:1-7). Discuss this paradox as a group.

6. In chapter 4 of *We Speak*, Mike writes about boasting. Read 2 Corinthians 12:9-10 and discuss the focal point of our boasting in Christ. What does Paul mean when he says, "For when I am weak, then I am strong"?

7. Compare 2 Corinthians 12:9-10 with Jeremiah 9:23-24. What does this tell us about our source of power?

8. Which of the daily readings was most helpful for you this week? Why?

9. Share with the group about a strength of yours that can be a barrier to trusting in the strength of Christ. What part of your qualifications needs to be surrendered to the sufficiency of Christ?

Give

10. At the conclusion of the video teaching today, we referenced the piercing question that Jesus asked the Pharisees: "What do you think about the Christ? Whose son is he?" (Matthew 22:42). Regardless of our accomplishments, we are called to share about the Logos, the Son of God.

11. As a group, compile a list of as many titles, attributes and descriptions of Jesus as you can gather in five minutes. Search what you already know to be true of him, check

online and look in your Bibles. Redistribute this list to the group later in the week.

Go

12. Conclude your meeting by praying together as a group. Consider addressing Jesus by the many attributes and titles you just shared as a group. Ask for strength and wisdom to share about the Logos with those who will listen—and even if nobody is listening.

13. Continue reading the daily devotionals in preparation for next week's discussion and application.

We Speak of
Hope in Suffering

Gather

Choose one of these discussion starters to launch the group
into a discussion about how "we speak of hope in suffering."

- Which would be hardest to lose 10 percent of in the next
  month: your income, your sleep, your food or your free time?

- Do you anticipate increased prosperity or decreased prosperity in the next twenty years in our country? Explain.

Grow

1. Invite the group to begin the study by praying together.
   Consider starting the prayer by addressing Christ with his
   titles and attributes shared last week.

2. Watch the video for week 5, "We Speak of Hope in Suffering." Add to the following highlights as you note insightful or important comments.

- "*Pneuma* is the word that explains today how God speaks. It's one of those words that . . . it's a bit elusive for some Bible readers. . . . [It's] probably good to start by just saying that the word *pneuma* literally means 'wind' or 'breath.'" J. K. Jones

- J. K. paraphrased a quote famously attributed to A. W. Tozer: "If the Holy Spirit was withdrawn from the church today, 95 percent of what we do would go on and no one would know the difference. If the Holy Spirit had been withdrawn from the New Testament church, 95 percent of what they did would stop, and everybody would know the difference."

- "If we try to run churches in our own power, if we try to witness in our own power, then . . . it becomes ineffective because the Holy Spirit's not in it. So . . . more than ever we need to rely on the Holy Spirit." Mike Baker

3. Did anything surprise or inspire you in this week's video teaching? Explain.

4. Acts 1:8 highlights the word *pneuma*, which was discussed in this week's video teaching. Even the disciples needed power from the Holy Spirit to accomplish the work God had in store for them. When it comes to depending on the Holy Spirit today, are we more often reliant or reluctant? Explain.

5. How much of our activity in the church depends on the power of the Spirit? Would things change if the Spirit withdrew from the church?

6. Seasons of suffering tend to highlight our level of co-operation with the Holy Spirit. When you are in your most

difficult times of pain and suffering, do you tend to rely on God or do you resist him? Explain.

7. In this week's reading, Mike talks about hope in the midst of suffering in four categories:

  • suffering from poverty

  • suffering from poor health

  • suffering mentally and emotionally

  • suffering from persecution

Which of these areas of suffering is most common in your life?

8. In the daily readings, J. K. talks of various areas of hope from 1 Peter:

  • a prepared hope (3:15)

  • a living hope (1:3)

  • a battle-ready hope (1:13)

  • a grounded hope (1:20-21)

  • a fulfilled hope (5:10)

Which of these elements of hope is most frequently expressed in your life?

Give

9. Have someone in the group document the kinds of suffering and hope that were discussed in the previous two questions. Hold onto this list as you begin praying for one another to display authentic hope in the midst of suffering.

10. As a group, try to summarize how the Spirit's power intersects with hope for the Christ-follower.

Go

11. Conclude your meeting by praying together as a group. Have three to four people pray for the specific suffering and hopes discussed during the meeting.

12. Continue reading the daily devotionals in preparation for next week's discussion and application.

We Speak
Throughout Our Lives

Gather

Select one of these discussion starters to get the conversation going in your group today.

- Share an example of an older, wiser person you've learned from in the past or present.

- Does our society over-esteem children and under-esteem the elderly? Explain.

Grow

1. Invite someone to lead the group in prayer, inviting the Holy Spirit to teach and instruct through your discussion.

2. Watch the video for week 6, "We Speak Throughout Our Lives." Add to the following highlights as you note insightful or important comments.

   - "People will say things like, 'I love Jesus, but I don't

want anything to do with the church.' New Testament writers would never divorce those two." J. K. Jones

- "This is the place where we grow, where the teaching takes place of the Word of God, we encourage each other with the grace of Jesus Christ, and we use our gifts. All generations, young, old, no matter who you are, no matter what you've done—you have a voice in the church of Jesus Christ." Mike Baker

- "We are not perfect people, and we declare it from Scripture. That's why we need a Savior. And so I heard this phrase many years ago that I really loved—that we are the most sincere hypocrites you'll ever want to meet. The truth is . . . we really want to be perfect followers of Jesus Christ, but we mess up. And so you should feel welcome to the church because it's a place for imperfect people." Mike Baker

3. There was a lot of information covered in this video teaching. Was there anything said that should be reiterated?

4. Based on your experience, do people tend to reject Christ or Christians? To say it another way, are people more likely to resist the message (of Christ) or the messenger (the church)?

5. In chapter 6 of *We Speak*, Mike noted, "Every generation is designed to function in and speak into the life of the church. Yet it can often be hard for a generation to find its voice, and this is mostly felt for the generations on either end of the age spectrum—namely, the young and the old." How does our church address this challenge and opportunity?

6. As a group, read 1 Timothy 4:12. Does our congregation expect this kind of example from those who are younger?

7. Read Psalm 71:17-18 as a group. What does this passage suggest about those who are elderly?

8. In your opinion, which of the following life stages presents the greatest challenges for speaking into the life of the church?

   - Youth: zero to twenty years *listen more now*
   - Young adult: twenty-one to forty years
   - Middle aged: forty-one to sixty years
   - Older: sixty-one to eighty years
   - Elderly: eighty-one and beyond

Give

9. Think about your social interactions. What wisdom do you extend to those who are younger than you? Are there older people in your life who share their wisdom with you?

10. In what ways can your group serve those of a different generation in the coming month or two?

Go

11. In what ways can your group become more intentionally influenced by other generations as you move forward? What can you leave behind for the next generation?

12. Continue reading the daily devotionals in preparation for next week's discussion and application.

We Will Never Stop Speaking

Gather

Choose one of the discussion starters below to begin a conversation about how "we will never stop speaking." Make sure everyone has an opportunity to contribute in the discussion.

- Describe the biggest talker you've ever known. What is his or her favorite topic?

- As a group, talk about what you've learned about each member of the group through this study. Be careful to mention at least one detail about each member.

Grow

1. Take a moment to pray together, asking God to guide and direct the group through this final week of *We Speak*.

2. Watch the video for week 7, "We Will Never Stop Speaking." Add to the following highlights below as you note insightful or important comments.

- "His mission was to fulfill Scripture, and his teaching always upheld Scripture. He never disrespected, never disregarded, never disagreed with any of Scripture. He affirmed every bit of law, every prophecy, every narrative, every poetic piece. He believed that the Bible was all true and all edifying and all important and all about him." J. K. Jones, paraphrasing Kevin DeYoung, *Taking God at His Word*.

- "The Word says of itself that it's living and active, sharper than any two-edged sword. The Word says of itself that it will not return unless it accomplishes what God set out to do in it. And so, God says, Here's this written word, this powerful thing, you can use to share your faith about Jesus Christ with others. . . . Quote the Scriptures because they speak of Jesus Christ." Mike Baker

- "Jesus often started the Scriptures by saying, 'It is written,' and that was his way of saying, 'This is authoritative. This is what I have to say.' And you know what? Maybe in the back of our minds, [when] we share our faith with our friends, with our family, with our neighbors . . . we should keep that phrase [in mind] . . . because we have this resource, the written Word of God that declares the truth of Jesus Christ." Mike Baker

3. Did you take any additional notes during the video this week? What did you find helpful?

4. As a group, read Acts 5:12-42. Be careful to note how the apostles spoke of Jesus even when they were repeatedly warned against such talk.

5. If you had been with the apostles at that time, would the threats have silenced you? Why or why not?

6. In what ways do we experience an attempted silencing of the Christian message in our culture today?

7. Read each of the primary passages from J. K.'s daily readings this week (Acts 1:8; 4:29; 5:42; 6:7; 26:27-29). What do you hear about their commitment to communicating truth?

8. In Friday's reading, J. K. wrote, "Where does persuasive gospel-speech find its source? The answer is simple. When people meet Jesus and become convinced that he is the sovereign Lord of the universe, they are forever incapable of keeping it to themselves." Do you agree?

Give

9. In our video teaching today, we were challenged to respond in three ways:

   - know the Scriptures
   - apply the Scriptures
   - trust the Scriptures

While each of these requires a lifetime of discovery, in the following appendix we've laid out a simple challenge for the next nine months.

10. Which of these seven weeks of teaching has been most helpful to you? Why?

Go

11. Conclude your meeting by praying together as a group.

Pray for one another to know the Scriptures, apply the
Scriptures and trust the Scriptures with all wisdom, humility and courage.

12. Discuss any future studies and commitments as a group.

Acknowledgments

In his whimsical and penetrating book *Listening to Your Life*, Fred Buechner tells the strange and brief story of Lyman Woodard. In 1831 Woodard's church was "repaired and several new additions were made. One of them was a new steeple with a bell in it, and once it was set in place and painted, apparently, an extraordinary event took place. . . . One agile Lyman Woodard stood on his head in the belfry with his feet toward Heaven."[1] Apparently due to a profound heart of gratitude and celebration Mr. Woodard couldn't contain himself and decided to stand on his head with his feet extended toward heaven. Mike Baker, Jim Probst and I resemble upside-down Lyman Woodard. If we could we would simultaneously stand on our heads and wiggle our toes toward heaven. We are immensely grateful! Let us count some of the ways.

Our partnership with IVP, especially Cindy Bunch and Jeff Crosby, has been exceptional. Our indebtedness to their expertise, wisdom and guidance is incalculable. The Eastview Christian Church staff also deserves our gratitude. They encouraged us all along the way, willingly took on additional projects that allowed us to focus on completing *We Speak,* and offered hundreds of prayers to our good and faithful heavenly Father on our behalf. Shawn Prokes, Nathan Baker-Lutz, Pete Wiedman, Jason Sniff and others were colossally helpful during the recording portion of this project. More than anyone or anything, we thank God for the support of our families and especially our wives, Sara, Julie and Sue. Never in a millennium could we do what God has called us to do without their love and selflessness. It is with Lyman Woodard joy that we acknowledge all the good ways God in Christ has made *We Speak* possible. All the praise is his and all the mistakes are ours.

Appendix

Verses for Future Study

Commit to memorizing one verse per month over the next nine months while looking for ways to demonstrate trust in his Word as you apply it to your daily life and conversations. Here are the verses to read collectively as a group and then memorize individually:

What is Scripture?

- 2 Timothy 3:16 *November*
- Hebrews 4:12
- Romans 15:4

What is good news?

- John 3:16-17
- Romans 5:8-11
- Titus 2:11-14

How are we to speak?

- Ephesians 4:25
- Matthew 22:42
- Acts 5:42

Notes

Introduction

[1]Christian Chronicler, "Campbell's Great Debate," christianchronicler .com/History2/campbell_debates.html.

[2]www.acu.edu/sponsored/restoration_quarterly/archives/1990s/vol_37_ no_1_contents/holloway.html.

Chapter 3: We Speak Even If No One Listens

[1]Blue Letter Bible, s.v. "*nabaʾ*," ESV, Hebrew Lexicon, Strong's H5012, www.blueletterbible.org/lang/lexicon/lexicon.cfm?Strongs=H5012&t =ESV (accessed July 18, 2014).

Chapter 4: We Speak Powerfully in Weakness

[1]Strabo, *Geography* 8.6.20, trans. Horace Leonard Jones, Loeb Classical Library 196 (Cambridge, MA: Harvard University Press, 1984).

Chapter 5: We Speak of Hope in Suffering

[1]Frank E. Gaebelein, gen. ed., *The Expositor's Bible Commentary*, vol. 12 (Grand Rapids: Zondervan, 1981), p. 212.

[2]Valentina Pasquali, "The Poorest Countries in the World," *Global Finance*, www.gfmag.com/global-data/economic-data/the-poorest-countries-in -the-world (accessed November 14, 2014).

[3]Tom Heneghan, "Reported Christian 'martyr' death double in 2103: report," January 8, 2014, Reuters, www.reuters.com/article/2014/01/08/us -christianity-persecution-report-idUSBREA070PB20140108.

Chapter 7: We Will Never Stop Speaking

[1]Tom Murse, "5 Longest Filibusters in U.S. History," *About News*, http://
usgovinfo.about.com/od/uscongress/tp/Five-Longest-Filibusters.htm.
[2]Blue Letter Bible, s.v. "Acts 5:40," ESV, www.blueletterbible.org/Bible
.cfm?b=Act&c=5&t=ESV#s=t_conc_1023040 (accessed March 31, 2015).
[3]Ibid.

Acknowledgments

[1]Frederick Buechner, *Listening to Your Life: Daily Meditations with Fred-
erick Buechner* (New York: HarperCollins, 1992), p. 180.

Further Resources

Check out the North American Christian Convention website. The 2015 convention features sermons based on the themes of this book. They are archived at gotonacc.org.

Eastview Christian Church at eastviewchurch.net/wespeak has an archive of sermons around the themes of the book as well.